Seeking Meaning
– Prayer as Quest

Ian Corbett and Chris Dunton

Seeking Meaning
– Prayer as Quest

Ian Corbett and Chris Dunton

Pendlebury Press Limited, 20 May Road, Swinton
Manchester, M27 5FR, U.K.

ISBN: 978-1-9999846-6-3

Ian Corbett

Chris Dunton

DEDICATION

To the Trustees, Warden's Team, St Leonard's
Church and all members of the Beauchamp
Community in Malvern, Worcestershire, for their
friendship and support, and for providing Ian Corbett
with a home.

Acknowledgements

Chris Dunton gives thanks for the love and friendship of those spiritual mentors he mentions in Chapter Three, and to the team leaders at the Greenhouse Christian Centre, Poole – Tom and Jessica Workman, and Mark and Kate Strand. Also to Tenny, his team leader on the Alpha Group he attended at St. Swithun's Church, Bournemouth. His essays are written in loving memory of the late Clement Mullinger of Lelapa la Jesu, Roma, Lesotho, and the late Father Dermot Tuohy of the National University of Lesotho.

Ian Corbett wishes to thank Tashi, Patrick, Richard and Motsoalle for all they have given him; the 'little people' of Lesotho and Navajoland who have nurtured him; and Chris Dunton for a journey in friendship and literature

We both acknowledge the patient persistence of Patsy Hughes, who persisted in deciphering Corbett's scribble for typing, and the generosity and willingness of Geoffrey Howard of Pendlebury Press in taking on all the work necessary to preparing the book for publication. To both of them go our sincerest thanks and appreciation.

CONTENTS

Preface

This book arose from troubled periods in both authors' lives, and this is reflected in the text. Then we were all overtaken by the horrors of the Covid pandemic, and, as I write now, by the barbarity of the war in Ukraine. In such circumstances we are often compelled to look deeper into our anxiety: Why do we suffer? Does life have meaning? Is there a God? Are we alone in a frighteningly huge, random universe? Our immediate concerns give rise to larger ones.

A first response is to look for comfort, or better, consolation. A marvellous new book by Michael Ignatieff, *On Consolation*, explores this theme by examining how some of the great thinkers and artists of the past have found reassurance. For Job in the Old Testament it is enough that, in the end, he is heard by God and makes his case. The candour and honesty of the Psalms unites us with a body of writing whose authors have been there before us and understand our predicament. Paul the Apostle did not live to see the great flowering of the Church for which he worked so assiduously but did come to realise the everlasting potency of the three great virtues of faith, hope and love. For some philosophers, such as Cicero, the approval and recognition of contemporaries was the justification of a life well lived, while for others the survival of their writings or their vision, or merely the knowledge life has been lived to the full and greatly enjoyed, has been sufficient consolation. For Abraham Lincoln a deep conviction that moral values lived out of experience were the necessary foundation of society, for Karl Marx a utopian vision he was confident was realisable, were ample rewards from life's journey. Nearer our own times holocaust and genocide have led survivors to try to find meaning in insisting we witness and remember those evils and accept responsibility, and for writers such as Camus to ponder now living 'outside grace', holding on to at least the possibility of experiencing the good.

Consolation is necessary and strengthening as we face the losses and disasters of life. But often we are led to go further. There may be a requirement to make adjustments in our lives in response to reverses we have suffered. In her latest book, *The White Stone*, Esther de Waal offers such insights. We may need to learn to let go – of possessions, certainty, and sometimes of people. Attachment can prevent us treading lightly through life, and can burden, inhibit or hinder our spiritual journey. Living more simply, and finding more time to be alone to enter more fully into our interior space, may become advisable. But there are two demands above all: to learn to practise mercy – to forgive, oneself as well as others – and to prepare for a certain diminishment as we grow older, to accept with humility that we cannot do all that we once did, and to do so without rancour but with grace and gratitude. These are demanding and costly processes.

But many of us will remain unsatisfied and struggle to ask even more difficult questions. Consolation, and adjustments in our life-style to enable further growth, are important, but still the mind and spirit ask – what is life, all this striving and hopefulness, for? What, if anything, comes next? Where is God? The most recent works of Richard Holloway, 'Waiting for the Last Bus', and 'The Heart of Things' are helpful here. First of all, we need to learn to accept life as it is, what we cannot change. We need to look again, to appreciate the beauty of the world and everything in it; and then to recall again, to remember with deep thanksgiving all the blessings of this life, and even what we have learned from its tragedies; and lastly, to forgive what needs to be let go of – personally, if possible but, if not, in our thinking. This is all part of 'befriending the stranger within', as he puts it, finally learning to love ourselves. Life passes, there are occasions to mourn, occasions to regret, but we can come to terms with it in a loving, forgiving acceptance.

You will notice that this retired bishop, while offering inexhaustible wisdom, does not speak of God or prayer. This is the dilemma we wish to explore further in this volume. Many of us in the church come to find that the usual response on offer – pray more fervently, God is in charge and will take care of everything, look forward to life beyond death – ring increasingly hollow. They don't seem to connect with the great realities already mentioned above – they can appear trivial and even flippant in the face of existential disaster. We find ourselves in an unimaginably vast, beautiful, complicated, dangerous universe, and our first response, as we find in the writers already quoted, should be one of wonder and humble inquiry. Those professing easy answers or undeniable truths should be treated with great suspicion. Religious systems pose considerable difficulties for us, compared especially with the teaching of their founders: such systems tend to develop and favour a systematic theology and an authoritarian structure that distort or ossify the original message. This is true of Christianity, Islam and, to a certain extent, Buddhism. They tend to oversimplify life issues so they become more manageable and answerable. Hence, in our time, while there is no lack in the West of spiritual interest, younger people are dropping out of organised religion. It can become a problem in exploring the world freely and finding our own pathways. In this book, two writers take this dilemma on board as they seek answers to those big questions posed at the outset.

We have to admit that there is much we do not know. The Eastern Orthodox will seek to talk of God only in negatives – He is not this or not that – for anything else will try to describe and therefore limit what God may be. In a recent book on 'Death and Dying', Canon Robert Reiss admits that most Western Christians probably now no longer believe in an individual after-life. Can there be, he wonders, a sort of 'resurrection of humanity' instead? So, we need to say here that no final or unambiguous answer can be given to what God is or how God exists, or to whether there is life after death or reincarnation. These are all tantalising possibilities. But it is important we pursue them not least because humankind is the better for doing so, in that compassion, self-sacrificial love, kindness and hope are encouraged and strengthened in this quest. The journey could be more important than any putative arrival. But the world is so full of clues and pointers to 'the transcendent in the midst' (I almost wrote 'mist') that many of us believe that the exploration <u>will</u> provide more answers <u>in the end</u> (one of the key phrases for our venture in this book).

Once we talk in terms of clues, impressions, voices, sights, understandings, rather than of rational answers or religious creeds, we are opening ourselves to the vital discovery that we can only answer our initial questions in terms of myth, imagery, and the arts, and that indeed scriptures themselves are to be understood not primarily as narrative texts or accumulated teaching but as myth and picture – the attempt, in fact, to describe the indescribable. So, it should not be a surprise to learn that none of the opening chapters of the Bible are literal fact but great stories that describe the deeply flawed nature of the human condition that the rest of the Bible addresses.

It should not be a scandal that the Early Church uses some of the stories associated with the Roman God Mithras in its trying to describe the miracles of the conception and resurrection of Jesus. And as we learn more of the influence of the Essene community on the New Testament, it could be that much more of it could be parabolic, that is reflection and story rather than literal fact in trying to convey the depth of the nature, teaching and impact of Jesus on his contemporaries. All theologians and philosophers must deal in myth, story and art to understand both scripture and religious experience. This is perhaps most clearly seen in the rich sagas of Hindu tradition and the elaborate Creation accounts of Native Americans.

As I will explain later, I tend to be aware of a Presence inhabiting the universe, who may or may not be its Creator. This is supported by much personal experience, reading and artistic immersion. My favourite image is that of the Welsh poet, R.S. Thomas, who finds God constantly elusive: he's just gone as you arrive, or he has hidden himself from our eyes. Yet for me the most tangible form of the presence of a God is in the Christian mass or eucharist, where the God descends to share Godself with all people. But this is clearly a mystery that I will try to explicate a little more later but perhaps can only more adequately be described by the organ music of Messiaen.

I can perhaps best illustrate where I am coming from and the direction of my travel by referring to another remarkable book, *The Shattering of Loneliness* by Erik Varden. He is a monk writing in a Christian tradition but I hope that both what he, I and Chris Dunton write, in that tradition, will speak beyond it to all who are seeking meaning in their lives at this critical time in our history.

The point of writing at all is because of the conviction that I share with Erik Varden that 'to become a man is to assume a great burden', that of trying to make some sense of the world for the sake of others. Like me, he has found inspiration and guidance in the music of Gustav Mahler, who wrote his own poem for the finale of his 'Resurrection' Symphony: -

> 'Have faith, heart, have faith: nothing will be lost to you.
> What you have longed for is yours, yes yours.
> Yours is what you have loved and fought for.
> Have faith: you were not born in vain.
> You have not lived or suffered in vain.'

This yearning I recognise as my own, just as I see the yearning in those elongated figures in El Greco's paintings, stretching up to heaven. I realised then that the burden of my life was to follow my heart in the searching for this hope, this promise, which could explain my whole life and world. I am still so engaged. I often get lost but then new disclosures come, my heart expands and a deep joy arises. That Presence I mentioned seems to be benevolent and apparently willing to be contacted, but also seems to be largely veiled and hidden. So, I must always probe, not give up, and therefore never be at ease. Cardinal Newman once preached 'to be at ease is to be unsafe'. But I am encouraged by one of those great narratives alluded to earlier: the account of Christ's Passion in the gospels – the God who saves by forgiveness even at the moment of crucifixion – is the only way of living, of spending a life, that makes any deep sense to me, immensely demanding though it is. So there has to be some absolute truth behind it. It is something to do with being open to what confronts you: a life closed in on itself cannot be fruitful. So, we should always look to the horizon, like astronomers scanning the heavens for signs of extra-terrestrial life. For our deepest desires and aspirations can carry messages from afar: 'they make us sick for a land we have not yet discovered. And that homesickness, that longing, invites us to enter a new kind of awareness'. So, says Varden, and I have to agree with him from my own experience. This gives me the confidence to hope that, through all the exploration that follows in this book, I shall be able to join in the following prayer of St. John Chrysostom. And if the 'Golden Mouthed' is not for you, then I trust you will find your own hope expressed in a similar way in whatever religion or philosophy speaks most to you.

'You have laid on me, O Christ, a spell of longing,
you have charmed me with a love all divine:
Consume, therefore, my sins with immaterial fire;
Be pleased to fill me with your sweet delights.
Then I shall magnify your advent in the past
and the one we still await with joy,
O Gracious God.'

ST. JOHN CHRYSOSTOM

1
Introduction

This book is a collaborative effort between Ian Corbett and Chris Dunton, who met in 1988 at the National University of Lesotho, at which time the former was the Warden of the Lelapa La Jesu Anglican Seminary on the University Campus, and Dunton was Professor in the University's English Department.

Years later, when Corbett published his spiritual/ pastoral memoir A Disreputable Priest (Gilead Books, 2015), Dunton reviewed it for the weekly Lesotho newspaper *thepost* [*sic*]. In that review, he drew particular attention to what Corbett had to say about prayer, as those parts of the book seemed to him especially inspired. At a point, when both he and Corbett were, after half a lifetime abroad, domiciled back in the UK and continued to meet, he suggested to his friend (and, by now, spiritual mentor) that he write a more extensive piece on prayer. Thus, the genesis of the present book.

Their friendship and their collaboration as authors notwithstanding, Corbett and Dunton have had very different career trajectories and—notably—a very different history in respect of faith.

Corbett was Birmingham born and bred before

attending the University of Cambridge, graduating in history and theology. He taught in schools prior to ordination and then served in the Diocese of Manchester. He did innovative and experimental work with youth (including with a chapter of Hell's Angels), with chaplaincy in Colleges of Further Education, and with in-service training of the clergy, becoming the youngest ever canon of the cathedral. He was invited through personal contacts to become the Warden of Lelapa la Jesu, the Anglican Seminary in Lesotho, while working covertly for the A.N.C. with refugees. In the nineties he did Christian education work in Botswana, Zimbabwe and South Africa but had his contract cancelled in the latter two because of his homosexuality (though no evidence of improper behaviour was produced). After two years' absence with myalgic encephelomyelitis (M.E.) he became Dean of Tuam in Eire, organising an international arts festival, before returning to 'coal face' work with indigenous peoples on reservations in Canada and the United States, his work being recognised by a Humanities Award from the State of Utah.

The opportunity to work in so many different cultures has enabled him to experience very varied attitudes to sexuality and religion. For example, just as Christianity in Lesotho tends to be binitarian (the Father and the Son brought in to close alignment) so do many males tend towards bisexuality (though the homosexual element is identified as a close form of friendship rather than of sexuality, even if sexual expression is involved). Again, in some Native American world views, Christian theology and traditional worship can either be combined, or experienced separately without any sense of contradiction, while more than two sexualities are acknowledged by some First Nations and 'two spirit' people are honoured, some being shamans. This accommodation of other approaches with his own tradition informs Corbett's thinking, so his work on prayer is influenced by his experience and, he hopes, speaks to people of varied backgrounds.

Dunton, by contrast, is a lifelong left-wing socialist who studied Literature at Oxford University, where he was a member of Terry Eagleton's Marxist Study Group. His only significant contact with people of faith was his friendship with Eagleton, a devout Catholic, amongst whose many books is one entitled *The New Left Church*, and with members of the radical Blackfriars religious community. An especially happy memory from those years is of listening to a Labour Party election manifesto speech on television and of one of Blackfriars' team leaders pointing to the screen and muttering: "come on, I dare you to utter the word 'socialism'"

Forty years in Africa followed, with Dunton becoming a professor specialising in African literature. Over time he read and re-read parts of the Bible, finding inspiration in the Psalms and Gospels. A less happy experience was reading the book of Ezekiel, in order to get to grips with the account of the Valley of Bones, which provides a major trope for

African liberation poetry; although the relevant passage is astoundingly beautiful, Dunton hadn't realised it comes towards the end of the book, preceded by 36 chapters of excoriation.

He has written extensively on sexualities in Africa and was a pioneer in the study of the representation of homosexuality in African literature. During his time in Lesotho, he was a leading member of the LGBTQ+ support group Matrix, meetings of which were held – significantly for Dunton, given his later trajectory – at St. John's Anglican Cathedral, Maseru.

Returning to the U.K. in 2016 and finding himself homeless, Dunton was blessed to be surrounded by men and women of faith. First came the experience of making friendships and sharing worship with the staff and guests of the Greenhouse Christian Centre in Poole; then, crucially, the experience of attending the Alpha group convened at St. Swithun's Church, Bournemouth. Amongst writers on faith who have been especially important to him are Michael Mayne, Ann Persson and Henri Nouwen. It is from this position that he is able to contribute to the present book. We should like to point out that the book is not merely a compilation but a collaborative effort, with the two authors reviewing each other's work to enable a unified approach to its composition.

As Corbett and Dunton came to know each other, working on the campus of the National University of Lesotho, they became aware both of each other's sexuality and of their involvement in the politics of the Left. Corbett had been a founding member of Bolton Free Press, Manchester Gay Liberation Front and the Manchester Gay Christian Movement. Under wise and sensitive bishops in Manchester at the time he had been among the first to conduct Blessings of Gay Relationships, albeit privately, and was widely used in counselling. Coming to Lesotho was the first comfortable time in his relational life as he experienced both the spiritual friendships and relaxed sexuality of the Basotho. Because he is a priest in the Anglican Church most of his gay relationships have needed to be furtive and discreet. This has placed heavy burdens on him psychologically. His relationships in Zimbabwe and South Africa, necessarily secret, were effectively terminated by his expulsion from those countries. In all, his treatment by the Church has driven him to its very edges, and his relation to it is both peripheral and pessimistic. It does not embody the Love of which it speaks.

. . . . . .

These words were written at what turned out to be the onslaught of the covid pandemic, and their process into a published work was put on hold. Now, two years further on, both writers felt compelled to review their work and respond to it in light of further experience. Hence, Dunton has produced a further reflection on prayer and poetry, and Corbett has traced his continuing spiritual pilgrimage in a final chapter. We hope this evolutionary process will in itself encourage our readers to pursue their own journeys with renewed vigour.

2
Prayer

Ian Corbett

Once you accept the existence of God
- however you define Him   -
Then you are caught forever
With His presence in the centre of all things.
You are also caught with the fact that
Man is a creature who walks in two worlds
And traces upon the walls of his cave
The wonders and the nightmare experiences
Of his spiritual pilgrimage.

MADELEINE OWEN-WILLIAMS, 1983: quoted
in *The Church Times*

There is only one road
that can lead to God and this is fidelity,
to remain constantly true to yourself,
to what you feel is highest in you.
The road will open before you as you go…

What paralyses life is failure to believe
and failure to dare.
The day will come when,
after harnessing space,
the winds,
the tides
and gravitation,
We shall harness for God the energies of love
And, on that day, for the second time
In the history of the world,
we shall have discovered fire.

PIERRE TEILHARD de CHARDIN

i

Our life is a short ride in a fast machine, sometimes with intervals of a purgatorial drudge but more often either soaring to the heights of heaven or plunging to the depths of hell. It is an exploration into God, that is, a journey into meaning which hopes to discover a still centre to our tumultuous universe, which is the loving heart of its Creator. It is a pilgrimage to find the source of a truth usually apprehended only fitfully in moments of contemplation, wonder or transcendence, that "ultimate reality is gracious" (Paul Tillich). The essence of this quest is not to discover a heavenly architect: I am persuaded by much contemporary biology, physics and philosophy that the existence of the material world can be accounted for without reference to a divine being outside it, even though the term 'Creator' seems the most adequate picture of God (as in Native American theology). But my experience, together with the insights of all the main religions, particularly Eastern Orthodox Christianity, Hinduism, Yoruba, Khoisan and Navajo Spirituality, is that I sense a Presence indwelling this random universe which benignly seeks to communicate to us that meaning can be found in this chaos in terms of relationships – to 'God', to one another, and to all living beings. Prayer, I would assert, is the word which best describes this adventure – an attitude of caring attentiveness and loving reaction to what is received. We can never grasp this God with the intellect; He can never be known or the object of our knowledge, but He is always the source of our wonder. I have an ecstatic sense of this marvellous world in which we live, which points me to a cause. These eureka moments, times when 'the penny drops', the thin places, I will explore further in the second section.

For now, let me explain that the spiritual and intellectual framework of my exposition is a classic Christian one, though not far removed either from the Hindu concept of the avatar or the Navajo yei. I believe that Jesus of Nazareth is the person and focus in whom we see the nature of this indwelling presence most fully revealed. He so understood this nature, and lived so close to its heart, that he shone in reflecting this passionate love of God for the world. God, being in the formulation of the Holy Trinity, Himself pure relationship, cannot exist without being in communion with all He indwells. And that love is extraordinary beyond belief: it extends to everything, with a particular mindfulness of the most apparently insignificant, despised, ignored and forgotten creatures, human and animal; and it never abandons, hates or destroys, whatever our responses may be. This love is unconditional, relentless and indestructible. Even when Jesus is condemned for implicitly threatening the power structures of his day and undergoes torture and an agonising death, he never stops loving but continues to reveal the love of whom He understands as Father. This love will sacrifice itself to be true to itself, and the Resurrection is a symbolic proclamation that it will always endure, and is always available, and is the hope for reconciliation, the healing of human conflict, and the consummation of the universe. Merely to say, in the conventional way, that God incarnated Himself in Jesus so that human sin could be forgiven and the race given new hope, is to denigrate the unspeakable nature of this love. God would have made Himself known, would have reached out to us, come to us, even if Adam had not sinned, because that is His nature. God cannot be alone. He needs us as we need Him. Above all, He suffers with us. It is the profound insight of Thomas in John's Gospel that the Risen Christ must bear upon His body the marks of crucifixion. If they had been absent, it would have suggested that God in Christ had not been permanently affected, even changed, by the experience of the Incarnation. But He bears for ever those marks. The crucifix speaks of a God nailed to His throne. And it is precisely this most costly loving that can sustain us and enable us to dare to hope even in our most straitened circumstances.

The issue of suffering in the world is the greatest objection to belief in a deity, the problem of theodicy, justifying the works of God to man. God does not will suffering, but it is existentially endemic in the sort of universe in which we live, a world that is evolving. It has been said that this vast universe is just big enough to permit the possibility of the random conjunction of events which produced life. It necessarily entails pain, such as that implicit in natural selection and explicit in the outcomes of volcanic eruptions, hurricanes, tsunamis, disease and accidents. Most other suffering is caused by human selfishness, malevolence and lust for power. But these are all necessary evils in the sort of world we inhabit. God, loving us, shares these experiences and brings us through them. To the question, 'Where is God?' we answer, in the eye of the storm, in human tragedy. Moreover, if God is Love, and love depends on mutual giving and receiving, He cannot always be prescient in His dealings with us but rather responds to us as we change, suffer and grow. I believe God Himself learns, grows, develops through this interaction, He who is perhaps the Spirit driving onwards our evolutionary journey.

The consequences of Love being at the centre of the universe are both joyful and terrifying, joyful because such a Presence offers us hope in an otherwise meaningless or repugnant universe, terrifying because we are called, I believe, to let it so shape our lives that we become ourselves lesser revelations of this love to the world, to become, in the words of the closing Thanksgiving of the Anglican Eucharist, a 'living sacrifice'. He calls us to follow.

So, what are the means by which we may know Him, interact with Him, and respond to His need for us? For me, primarily the practice of prayer and worship, but also through the insights of the arts, and especially the natural world and the web of human relationships. Let us begin to look at these.

There are two directions by which we can investigate prayer. One is to regard it as a continuous movement of God towards us, a constant pouring out of the Holy Spirit into our hearts who then completes a recurring circular motion by taking our thoughts, aspirations and anxieties back into the loving heart of God. The second direction is from the human end of the relationship, regarding prayer as our search for God and our wish for knowledge of and fellowship with Him. Theologically, the first direction is primary but I will start with the second as it offers more possibility of common ground and experience – 'fides querens intellectum', faith seeking understanding.

ii

It may seem absurd to start this section talking about sex, but that is how it must be! For my recent experience in relationship is critical to my current state of prayer.

Eight years ago, I met a friend I had been waiting for all my life – at the ripe old age of 72! I had given up on ever finding such a person. I had subscribed to the old theory that a priest should remain unpartnered (I could never admit celibate!) so that, in the absence of a primary relationship, he could be available to all who need him. Psychologically, that position has all the flaws I now recognise, and we can probably all think of celibate priests who have withered from within for lack of love and intimacy. However, a brief affair that followed upon celebrations of my 70th birthday encouraged me to make one last attempt – on-line! And it was a triumph. When Tashi first came to see me, it was as though we had known each other for years and we soon came to accept and love each other completely. This was the more remarkable in that he was only in his early twenties, but astonishingly mature and understanding. He was all I could have wanted – beautiful, intelligent, humorous and intensely caring – and we had mutual interests in travel, music and philosophy. We never lived together as he was a student, eventually embarking on a Ph.D. course, and I dwelt in an almshouse community, but we talked every day, met at least once a week, and took holidays together. I had never felt so completely loved and accepted despite my many flaws, including my irritability, self-defensiveness and sensitivity to criticism; and we both felt passionately about each other. I had never been so happy.

But the age difference always threatened to become a problem. It was clear that Tashi was going to be spending most of his life with someone else. The issue was when that change would have to come. Tashi felt we should just carry on until we had to face the issue head on, occasioned perhaps by some marked deterioration in me. I was insistent that he must not sacrifice his life by looking after me in a degenerated state. So, the question became, would

Tashi decide a time would come when he felt the need to look elsewhere, or would I have to urge him to do this – rather like the Feldmarshallin in Richard Strauss' opera *Der Rosenkavalier*, who has to encourage her young lover to go to the much younger woman with whom his future must be! I knew Tashi would not look around while he was with me: we were both very loyal. In my 79th year I felt that I aged rather quickly and markedly, and indeed had almost collapsed on Tashi on one of our hikes. I was slowing down, losing energy, finding it harder just to keep up. We talked extensively, and we eventually agreed that perhaps now was the time for him to feel free to explore. He met someone fairly soon, and then, because of the lockdown consequent upon the coronavirus pandemic, was faced with the dilemma of living alone for an unspecified time or moving in with his new lover. He took a gamble and chose the latter. Fortunately, it has worked out well and they are both happy.

Now I want to stress that this happened with our joint agreement, perfectly loving and amicable and obviously I am relieved that he is happy and content. He could not have behaved better: he assures me we are to remain each other's best friends for ever, we still talk every day and meet once a week – and Patrick, the new man, bless him, is not threatened by this. Intellectually, I know we did the right thing, although the suddenness of Tashi's new arrangements were understandably a shock. But my emotions have received a blow from which I am finding it difficult to recover. No words are too excessive: I am devastated, lonely, lost and profoundly unhappy. I cry every day, but not the violent outpouring I feel I need to expel all the pent-up hurt and distress. I did not think it would be as shattering as this. Of course, God gets some blame: how could He have let the perfect partner into my life to then inflict this suffering on me? I know the time will come when I will be able to thank Him for letting me experience such bliss and ecstasy for six years at my age, but not yet. I found some release in composing a short sequence of poems which form the fourth part of this volume.

What reinforces my reaction is that all the close relationships I have allowed myself over the years have been snatched away from me. I was late in publicly acknowledging my sexuality, and quite timid in expressing it, but one of my friends in Bolton told me years later that, if I had only been more overt and intentional, he would have been happy to respond and spend his life with me. In Manchester, Richard was wonderful but bisexual, and increasingly heterosexual, so we eventually had to part, though at least we had lived with each other. Then, in Lesotho, Motsoalle, like all good African men, eventually married – but still felt he should be able to come round and spend nights with me! This is a not untypical situation with the Basotho, who see same-sex relationships more as close friendships than sexual relationships, even if sex is involved. But I had been his best man (rather surprising the Catholic priest) and was very fond of his wife, and could not accept this proposal. In both Zimbabwe and the Northern Cape, promising relationships were scuppered by my falling foul of bishops who cancelled my contracts (not over the particular relationships but over wider matters). I experienced no such possibilities while working with Native Americans later.

It began to seem as though God was letting me experience some deep consolation, but then withdrawing it, as though to say, 'I need all your attention to be on the tasks I have for you'. This feeling was reinforced by the pattern my career seemed to be taking, a process of being continually pared down and refined for some future project. Coming from a middle-class background, and having enjoyed an elite education, I experienced what I call my 'conversion to people' when teaching in problematic comprehensive schools in Coventry and Birmingham, realising the extraordinary personal riches that are to be found in the most disadvantaged people. As a priest in Bolton, I worked with teenagers involved in gangs and drugs, and again was struck by how they befriended me as much as I them. In Manchester, I was educated in an alternative British history by the director of the West Indian Centre, now discovering God in other peoples and religions. Then as Director of Clergy Training for the Diocese of Manchester I had the hard task of trying to equip priests for challenging and changing conditions. These were all qualities I needed when I was called to go out to Lesotho and be the Warden of the Seminary, Chaplain to the University, Director of Clergy Training and Parish Priest of the Roma Valley – four posts really, in a country surrounded by apartheid South Africa.   Later, I had immense difficulties in tackling demanding training posts in Zimbabwe, Botswana and South Africa, exacerbated by unreasonable bishops, but laboured on till my health failed.   Work in the first decade of the present century with First Peoples in Canada and the United States brought me to even more demanding work with people who were absolutely traumatised and lost, often suffering consequently from disease and substance abuse.   It was as though, through all these years, God was constantly stripping me down for the next task, which was to be more demanding, until I had nothing left.   For two years after my time in Africa I was out of work with myalgic encephalomyelitis (M.E.), but even then, He demanded more, and I became dean of a cathedral in a struggling area of Ireland before crossing the Atlantic to work in North America, which I also had to leave for health reasons, though beyond retirement age, now having also contracted post-traumatic stress disorder (P.T.S.D.) and acquired a stent in my heart.   I departed a burnt-out case, nurtured at least among the Navajo by the extraordinary natural world in which they live and the vitality of their own religion and experience of God. I learned that all serious efforts to come close to the Creator must involve suffering, from the sweat lodge to the extremes of the Sun Dance.

This lengthy autobiographical narrative is necessary to explain why I was compelled to pose the question, was God really at work in the progress of my life as I have suggested, persistently removing my defences and comforts that I may become more vulnerable both to Him and to those whom I serve? Is this how He works? And, in my case, I think the answer is yes, as it must be to a greater or lesser extent in the lives of us all. The discovery I have only recently come to make in retrospect is this. WE NEED TO BE BROKEN OPEN FOR GOD TO BE ABLE TO ENTER OUR LIVES. This is a prerequisite of real prayer. For much of my life I have been trying to do God's work for Him, in my own strength, and often failing. It has taken me a lifetime to learn, with His incessant purging of my being, that prayer requires time and space, to be still, to listen, to receive. And God has had a hard time getting me to do this. Henri Nouwen has been an invaluable guide here, particularly his books *The Inner Voice of Love* and *The Wounded Healer*.

This is a very difficult lesson to learn for those of us who are serious about prayer. God needs to hollow us out so He can fill us with Himself. This is a long and often painful process as we naturally resist being taken in a direction we may not automatically choose, being asked to surrender aspects of our lives we wish to indulge but which will prevent the God of Love entering us, making His home in us. We would rather be ravished by sensual delights than by Him.

Now Tashi was not a barrier to this happening to me: rather he was a channel by which I came to know Love more deeply. But the God of Love wants me for Himself, and then to turn me outwards to others that suffer as a bearer of His love. Learning to receive Him is akin to the process of grieving: being prepared for Him may entail losses so great as to cause emotional and physical pain; we undergo periods of anger, isolation and hopelessness, and become more aware of our vulnerability and helplessness. But as we let go, He receives and nurtures us and we learn to make new connections and accept His grace, the ever-flowing source of our loving.

Yet we do not enter the Promised Land without going through the Wilderness. One shock we may encounter is that an AWARENESS OF GOD'S EXISTENCE MAY COME TO US MORE BY A SENSE OF HIS ABSENCE THAN HIS PRESENCE. Since my own trials I do not necessarily have a more frequent sense of Emmanuel, God-with-us, but rather a feeling that He has been here but recently departed, that He is a deepening shadow just out of sight, that He is like the silent house where only the twitching of a curtain suggests an occupant. A sense of absence is as much evidence of His being as a sense of Presence, and though I glimpse Him more by inference I become even more convinced of His reality. Moreover, the unfathomable depths of the Divine that I now discover make me realise that MY OWN DEPTHS HAVE TO BE PLUMBED FOR

PRAYER TO BE ACTIVE AND EFFECTIVE. The real prayers are when circumstances draw out of our inner being such exclamations as 'God help me' (I have no reserves left and throw myself on your mercy); 'Thank God' (I am overwhelmed by an experience of beauty, release or connection); 'God, I'm sorry' (the prayer of sorrow and penitence). Similarly, 'How wonderful'; 'I'm through' (the prayer of anxiety, despair or exhaustion), 'the pity of it', as Othello says. PRAYER IS A HUNGER FOR REALITY, both to face it and refer it to the Source of Healing. The French philosopher Péguy writes: 'you didn't come into the world to be a success; you came into the world to have a great heart and to suffer'.

I will turn to the consolations of prayer later. Here I want to point out that God trains us and offers Himself not only for our own growth and development but that we may become part of His Mission to His world, to assuage human suffering and to reveal His loving involvement and concern, nothing less than the remaking of humanity in His image; and that involves sharing in the carrying of His cross as Paul describes. It was a revelatory insight of Thomas to ask to see the wounds of the Risen Christ, as mentioned above. If the divine body had been unblemished, it would have suggested that God had not been permanently affected by the experience of Incarnation and Crucifixion. However, the wounds of Christ demonstrated that God was forever marked by his undergoing and knew, understood, shared the suffering experience of humanity, and were its only answer. With this God in us, and with the joy of this unconquerable love, we can accept that THE PLACE GOD CALLS US TO IS THE PLACE WHERE OUR DEEPEST CONCERN AND GLADNESS AND THE WORLD'S HUNGER MEET. Or, as Gandhi said, 'be the change you wish to see in the world'. Our growing awareness of Christ-in-us in prayer will therefore direct us towards the imperative of living for others.

St. Antony said, 'our life and death is with our neighbour; if we win our brother we win God, but if we cause our brother to stumble, we have sinned against Christ'. Our own spiritual life depends on dying to ourselves so we may put our neighbour in touch with Christ. St. Antony adds, 'the neighbour is our life; to bring connectedness with God to the neighbour is bound up with our own connection to God'. We are called to be part of the universal struggle of all those who believe it is wrong to inflict wrong on others. So our GROWTH IN THE SPIRITUAL LIFE IS INEXTRICABLY BOUND UP WITH OUR SERVICE OF THE WORLD'S GREAT NEED, because then the Christ in us is reaching out to the Christ in all of hurting humanity to participate in the Warfare of God, the battle against greed, corruption, violence, selfishness, aggression, hate, neglect, indifference and all those wickednesses which make a hell out of heaven for the majority of people in His world. And the only weapon that can be effective is a love that cannot be defeated, that love of God which we have been trying to let him grow in our hearts.

The realisation of this may take years of WAITING – waiting not with hope as we may expect the wrong things, as T.S.Eliot has pointed out, but with openness – waiting for the God who comes.

The demanding process we have been considering can be encouraged by the exercise of certain practices which complement our inner growth and are also the fruit of it. One necessity is the STUDY OF SCRIPTURE, preferably with a good commentary, which focuses us on the life and teaching of Jesus, and, in the Old Testament, the religious experience and development of an entire people. Another is summed up in LOVE OF MY NEIGHBOUR. Learning to put first God, then others, first in our lives before ourselves is a hard discipline. But, as Pope Francis always reminds us, attention to those most marginalised in our society is the litmus test of faith; or, as St. James tells us, 'faith without works is dead'. Issues of justice and freedom for all peoples should frequently concern us, in intercession, in almsgiving and in practical service. St. Isaac of Syria writes, 'Do not presume to call God just: for what sort of justice is this – we sinned, yet He gave up His Only-begotten Son on the Cross?' Because we receive more than justice from God – unending forgiveness and mercy – we must surely respond to the needs of the world as best as we are able. Equally demanding is Jesus' command to LOVE OUR ENEMIES, for only love can overcome hate. St. Antony said, 'Where the Spirit of the Lord is, there is love for enemies and prayer for the whole world'. More arrestingly he adds, 'keep your mind in hell, and despair not'. Share the suffering of whom Luke calls the 'anawim', the little ones, the lost ones, those whom Frantz Fanon called 'the wretched of the earth', and stay with them until hope is born: sometimes we are called to live 'on the wrong side of the tracks' with the forgotten ones.

Another important consideration, which both arises from prayer and sustains prayer, is to compose a simple RULE OF LIFE making time for work, prayer, worship, relaxation, and sleep, and monitoring expenditure and life-style. The old monastic rules are useful guides to holy living, such as St. Francis' commendation of a life of poverty, humility, simplicity and prayer, or St. Benedict's rule of poverty, stability, and 'conversion of manners' (that is living charitably with others). Note that humility and lack of extravagance are seen by both as key elements in our growth.

Now so far I have perhaps made prayer seem a very tough struggle and perhaps little else. But we are about to consider next the reckless abundance of God's love which is constantly enveloping us and fills us with joy. And for some, growth in prayer is not so difficult. But I wanted to emphasise the qualities of perseverance and persistence as most people make do with a mere reflection of what the intensity of prayer can be, turning God on and off like a tap, regarding Him as a sort of mate who can be approached casually, and ignoring Him for most of the time until we are in distress or want something. Like all the worthwhile things in life – friendship, marriage, achievement in our work or the arts – it requires discipline, obedience and hard work: only then does the joy and freedom flow. So now let us turn to the mystery of God's movement towards us.

iii

The genius of the Christian doctrine of the Trinity is that it expresses God as a community. This is brilliantly captured in Rublev's famous ikon of the Trinity, which depicts three identical figures seated around a table or altar, hands gesturing to one another as though flowing into one another. The table represents the eucharistic altar and/or the world, placed at their centre. Their heads and upper bodies could be enclosed in a circle, the symbol of eternity. So these aspects of Godhead – the Father (Creator), the Son (the revelation of the Father) and the Spirit (the presence of God with us now) – continually emit a stream of compassionate energy that takes us up into the loving heart of God in a sort of circular motion. This motion is also seen in the particular mission of the Son, emanating from the Godhead to become incarnate, crucified and risen and ascended, thereby taking our humanity into that same Sacred Heart of God. Similarly, the traditions kept by the Church, the Body of Christ, are the work of the Spirit in history, making the love of God known in our different cultures. 'Tradition' is not a static burden to be merely passed on but a living Presence calling the faithful. God's will for us is nothing less than the beautiful medieval word 'engodding': both St. Irenaeus and St. Anselm assure us 'God became man so man may become God (or be 'engodded)'. And this will of the Father is incessantly communicated to us by His continual outpouring of love, drawing us to Himself. This is truly the gospel, good news. It is this joy and ecstasy of heaven which is the goal of our strenuous seeking in prayer, because, while this is what is offered, it has to be received. All relationships depend on response, conversation, mutuality. The problem with our relationship with God is that if He revealed Himself to us totally, we could not stand such glory: it would consume us in the heat of its love. That is why Moses was allowed only to glimpse the rear of God as He passed. We could not withstand His direct gaze. So this kind and humble God reveals Himself to us in small ways that we can take in. But the point of our discipline in prayer is that we need to be ready to apprehend such revelations when they come. If Moses had not prepared himself by his hidden years in the desert, would he perhaps not have noticed the burning bush? We find God by being attentive to the world around us, part of the point of the discipline of prayer. I sometimes think that 'not noticing' is the true original sin, particularly when applied to people.

The inference of all this is we see God, in His revelation in Christ, and especially on the Cross, turning the traditional language of prayer upside down. We see GOD INTERCEDING FOR US, rather than our praying to Him, and GOD SACRIFICING HIMELF FOR US, rather than our making sacrifices to placate Him. This is why we can have the confidence that all our persevering in prayer will culminate in foretastes of His overwhelming love for us, in apprehensions of His glory and in a new hope beyond all present expectations or fears.

We may not be granted visions, like the Desert Fathers, or voices, like St. Joan, but we shall be granted evidences of His presence in the natural world, in other people, and in the intuitions of our hearts and minds. My first experience of God was, as a young teenager, a warm sense of presence in a time of extended unhappiness, a sort of assurance that has never left me, even in the darkest periods. This was reinforced by teaching in a comprehensive school in a very troubled urban area and finding that the loving acceptance of these wonderful but bruised young people seemed to be shadowed by something behind it, a sort of Presence loving them that drew unsuspected depths of affection out of them. For a time, I began to see halos round the heads of peoples – any person, even a baby! But the greatest of revelations of the God within us came during my work in Africa, when I came to realise that people who have very little in Western terms have everything that matters: when life is stripped back to the issues that are really central – family, friends, prayer, shelter, food, music, laughter – they predominate and God shines through; in other words, when all our usual defences are down. I have never been more loved and accepted than by the rural poor of Southern Africa. And this presence of God amongst them is reflected in their vibrant worship. My most harrowing insight into what it may have been like for God to love us in the face of our rejection was when I spotted a sick and emaciated young man lying in the market in Kuruman in the Northern Cape. I felt called to lift him and carry him to my house – to the jeers and taunts of largely white standers by. I bathed him, held him and fed him. He said nobody had loved him like this before. I felt God to be very near, only just out of sight.

I am often aware of 'inner promptings', as when the draw towards ordination became irresistible as all other doors seemed to be closing; as when I felt compelled on a visit to Wanuskewin, a Cree holy site in Saskatchewan, to go out and 'tell my story', underlined by clouds above gathering in the shape of an eagle, apparently unnoticed by anyone else there. I often feel moved to visit or contact people, and normally there turns out to be a reason why, unsuspected, I was needed.

Tiny annunciations, little transfigurations, happen to me regularly in the natural world. My own 'burning bush' experience came while descending the Drakensberg escarpment in South Africa late one afternoon. As the sun set it sank into the bowl between the twin summits of Hodgson's Peaks, as they are known in English. The vision spoke to me of the priest's wafer being held over the chalice of Holy

Communion. My heart expanded. Indeed, often such experiences happen to me on the high places, perhaps because these are the only habitude of total silence and peace. I learned my love of fell and mountain hiking in the English Lake District. Pillar, a remote peak not visible from any road, was my first place of epiphany, reached after a snowy climb on a thrilling spring day. It was, above all, a moment of feeling at one with all around me, a deep sense of belonging and a wonderful sensation of the sheer ecstasy of creation. Such experiences were repeated on my first climbs in the Drakensberg – Mont-aux-Sources, my first true mountain wilderness – and in the Rockies – Gray's Peak in Colorado, icy peaks retreating in all directions. The majesty of God is here certainly, but also His intimacy: 'do not be afraid'. Rocks that seem intimidating on the ascent I would touch as friends on the descent: after all, they had supported me! Native Americans taught me to be aware of such Presence elsewhere, too – in forests and rivers, in wind and storm, in animal life. I have had close experiences with elephants and cheetah in Africa and wolves in America that have equally conveyed the nearness of God and a unity in all things. In the remote ancient canyon dwellings of Utah, I used to hear voices and catch fleeting sightings of – people? I learned there is only a very thin veil separating the material and spiritual worlds. For trained eyes there are many 'thin spots'. I don't pray as regularly as I used to in terms of set times, but I have an almost continual sense of God within and around me. Is this what St. Paul means by 'praying without ceasing'?

To me, religion without art is unimaginable, and the arts furnish a profound route into God's presence. Who can read Dostoyevsky's *The Brothers Karamazov* without being changed? Or see the portraits of El Greco or view landscape through the eye of Monet? Or hear the Bach Passions or the symphonies of Mahler or Bruckner? These are works of the imagination that challenge and reshape our realities. And not only the great masterpieces: a Beatles song may be as profound as Schubert, a rap recital as a great drama. Because the subject of all that is written here is, strictly speaking, beyond words: the arts can express our experience where words fail.

Walking, too, can be revelatory, especially when done alone. Psychologically it appears that exercise is good for troubled minds but, above all, we have time to think, to observe, just to be. Space and silence are at a premium in our crowded, rushing and noisy world, so God scarcely has a chance to get a word in edgeways, as it were. Yet He inhabits silence. In Mark 7, Jesus 'took him aside, away from the crowd'. Our spiritual journeys cannot be done on express trains.

SILENCE is ultimately the most important context for being able to appreciate that 'God is here'. In the Sayings of the Desert Fathers, Abbot Pambo refuses to speak to the visiting Archbishop of Alexandria, asserting 'if he is not edified by my silence he will not be edified by my speech'. God's silence is more powerful than words – especially when it is received in our silence. Perhaps we are afraid to give Him the time, but He will not overwhelm us: 'what is required by God of each person is regulated according to their capacity'. But we are also afraid of the silence because it leaves us to face ourselves without distraction, and we don't like what we see. Yet it is only by facing up to ourselves, looking at ourselves in the mirror, that we can reconcile with ourselves, and, by going down into our own depths, discover that, at the bottom of the well, we find not despair but God awaiting us. For He is that close, in our inmost being, waiting to be recognised, so He can, with our assent, commence to remake us from within in His own image. John the Dwarf said, 'We have put aside the easy burden, which is self-accusation, and weighed ourselves down with the heavy one, self-justification'. It has also been said that 'the Englishman takes pride in being a self-made man, thereby relieving God of a fearful responsibility'. Let go of all of this baggage: accept yourself. God loves us as we are. Let yourself be loved! Be vulnerable in His presence. Only His truth can free us. Conflict is to be met everywhere but so is patience and so is the help of God. Don't wish to be elsewhere or doing something else: we take our psyche wherever we go! I have learned to pray, upon the good advice of a wise confessor, Fr. Ivan, 'Lord, make me strong in this place'. Wherever we are in life, God is there, we can find silence, and the redeeming work can go on. 'You can even be a solitary in your mind when you live in the middle of a crowd'. Archbishop Rowan Williams has written: 'Where we are and who we are is the furnace where the Son of God walks... When we discover silence, we shall... very, very occasionally, catch a glimpse of the fire, the desert filled with flame'. Mozart said the most beautiful thing in music is silence.

. . . .

And so, we draw to a close our meditation on the Love of God and the means of realising it. The discipline is hard, but the reward beyond the telling. Now you and I persevere, above all in waiting, but eventually in journeying on in this lifetime's (and beyond) exploration into God. It will cost us, but if we do not share the suffering of God's world, and therefore of God Himself, we are not really engaging in the quest. The Rock that seems to threaten us may turn out to be the Rock that supports us. All prayer and revelation ultimately goes out into mystery. In the end, God cannot be understood, only loved. There are no answers. But He always gives us 'just enough' to be able to go on.

Disturb us, Lord, to dare more boldly –
To venture on wider seas
Where storms will show your mastery;
where losing sight of land,
We shall find the stars.

We ask you to push back
The horizons of our hopes;
And to push us into the future
In strength, courage, hope and love.

Attributed to SIR FRANCIS DRAKE, 1577

Quoted by MAGGI DAWN on her website

You make what is ultimate and beyond
brightness
secretly to shine in all that is most dark.
In your way, ever unseen and intangible,
you fill to the full with most beautiful
splendour
those souls who close their eyes that they may
see.
And I, please, with love that goes on beyond
mind
to all that is beyond mind,
seek to gain such for myself through this
prayer.

From *The Cloud of Unknowing,* 14th century

The Prayer of One Who Seeks God

O Christ, my Lord, again and again
I have said with Mary Magdalene,
'They have taken away my Lord
and I know not where they have laid him.'
I have been desolate and alone.
And thou hast found me again, and I know
that what has died is not thou, my Lord,
but only my idea of thee,
the image which I have made to preserve
what I have found, and to be my security.
I shall make another image, O Lord,
better than the last.
That too must go, and all successive images,
until I come to the blessed vision of thyself,
O Christ, my Lord.

GEORGE APPLETON

Prayer

Prayer the church's banquet, angel's age,
God's breath in man returning to his birth,
The soul in paraphrase, heart in pilgrimage,
The Christian plummet sounding heav'n and earth
Engine against th' Almighty, sinner's tow'r,
Reversed thunder, Christ-side-piercing spear,
The six-days world transposing in an hour,
A kind of tune, which all things hear and fear;
Softness, and peace, and joy, and love, and bliss,
Exalted manna, gladness of the best,
Heaven in ordinary, man well drest,
The milky way, the bird of Paradise,
Church-bells beyond the stars heard, the soul's
blood,
   The land of spices; something understood.

GEORGE HERBERT

POSTSCRIPT TO CHAPTER 2

Do these thoughts do anything to build bridges to those with whom I am passionately concerned to connect, those outside religious belief systems? We all have our own convictions, often claiming certain areas of knowledge in support. Perhaps we ought to claim traditions of wisdom rather than of knowledge, because they all help us to live meaningfully in a complex world, coping with human suffering, vulnerability, trauma and failure. Jesus incarnates wisdom, not knowledge, while nevertheless enduring rejection, suffering and crucifixion. He therefore embodies for us a model of coping with meaninglessness, incoherence, uncertainty and tragedy, a cultivation of resilience in the face of life's enigmas. He offers an enhanced capacity to live within our world and cope with its uncertainty and complexity, as well as our own frailty and failings. He enables us to confront glib and shallow responses, such as rationalism, 'positive thinking' or emotional fundamentalism. In his latest book, *Through a Glass Darkly : Journeys through Science, Faith and Doubt*, Alister McGrath, argues that life is complex and ambivalent and cannot be lived in a spirit of denial: darkness must be confronted, uncertainty and paradox accepted, quick and easy interpretations resisted. A reviewer summarised his argument by saying that wisdom demands we respect and embrace a deep mystery, something that transcends the boundaries of human comprehension. We see 'through a glass darkly', as St. Paul writes, and that is why we need to acknowledge our limited capacity to understand and the fragility of the truths on which we base our lives. This is why we need one another, with all our traditions of wisdom, religious and secular, for company and solidarity, holding on to our visions of reality and wisdom and learning from them, so these visions in turn hold us, encouraging us, in our own places, to probe and discover the depth of our humanity and insight. And in Jesus we see someone who has embodied this great wisdom, walked through the darkness, and blazed a trail we all can follow. I believe my understanding of prayer in this wide and diffuse sense can offer common ground for people of many different persuasions in their search for Truth.

3

The Language of Poetry and The Language of Prayer

Chris Dunton

Readers will have noticed that in his fine essay on prayer Ian Corbett quotes several poems. Madeleine Owen-Williams's "Once you accept the existence of God" and Pierre Teilhard de Chardin's "There is only one road" provide a substantial and powerful preface to the essay. Later in the piece we find poems by Francis Drake, George Appleton and George Herbert and an anonymous poem from the 14th century.

For Corbett, poetry is evidently an important source of insight and inspiration, but it is, too, a vehicle for his own expression. Shortly before composing his essay, Corbett produced a five-part poem sequence entitled "Poems of Love and Loss"— a work in which he meditates on the life experience recounted in section 2 of his essay (the poem sequence appears next in this volume).

Clearly Corbett has benefitted from one of the central lessons in Henri Nouwen's beautiful book *The Inner Voice of Love*, which teaches us not to become submerged in the pain we have experienced, not to become a prisoner of pain, but at the same time not to be so foolish as to pretend that that pain was never suffered. In his poem sequence, Corbett quotes Samuel Beckett's novel *The Unnameable*: "You must go on. I can't go on. I'll go on" and the sequence ends with the lines "I still wait / But a rumour of angels sustains me." The bridge to angels is, surely, prayer.

i

The last thing I want to suggest in this essay is that poetry and prayer have contesting claims on us. I shall, though, begin by arguing that poetry has a very distinctive role to play in our lives, quite unlike that of any other form of discourse, and I shall close by giving two examples of the relationship between the language of poetry and that of prayer. In between, there may be a certain amount of meandering (and this despite the fact that a former colleague of mine was always begging me to "cut to the quick"—a poetic phrase if ever there was one).

This is not to suggest there is any absolute distinction between poetry and prose, or to deny the potential beauties of the latter. Take, for example, the sermons of Lancelot Andrews (1555-1626), Bishop and theologian and the man who guided the translation team that produced the King James Bible. A great admirer of Andrews was the modernist poet T.S. Eliot, who, in his *For Lancelot Andrews: Essays on Style and Order* (1928) praised Andrews' "desire for clarity and precision" and the "often poetic structure" of his sermons. Eliot went on to say: "Andrews takes a word and derives the world from it; squeezing and squeezing the word until it yields a full juice of meaning which we should never have supposed any word to possess." Yet poetry, as distinct from prose, has a special role to play.

What is the point of poetry? Or how much point is there to it? What does it have to offer us that is so special? These are questions that were raised in 2020 in the UK, following the government's decision to downgrade the teaching of poetry in schools. Amongst the major British writers who protested the decision I shall quote two.

Michael Rosen reminded us that "poetry offers a view on the world that is playful, contemplative, mysterious, questioning, and one that is often interested in giving readers the chance to hold several different ideas at the same time."

The other British author I wish to quote is Melvyn Bragg, who argued that "while paintings fade and sculptures crumble, poetry endures in the collective memory. Indeed, when Percy Bysshe Shelley wrote his famous sonnet "Ozymandias", about a statue to a great king that had crumbled into the desert sands, he was nodding to this."

It may seem odd in such an essay as the present one to make so much of the work of the atheist revolutionary Shelley. But here is "Ozymandias" (1818), as it provides one of the finest demonstrations in the English language of the very specific way in which poetry works.

I met a traveller from an antique land
  Who said: "Two vast and trunkless legs of stone
Stand in the desert. Near them on the sand,
  Half sunk, a shattered visage lies, whose frown
And wrinkled lip and sneer of cold command
Tell that its sculptor well those passions read
  Which yet survive, stamped on these lifeless things,
The hand that mocked them and the heart that fed.
And on the pedestal these words appear:
  'My name is Ozymandias, king of kings:
Look on my works, ye mighty, and despair!'
  Nothing beside remains. Round the decay
Of that colossal wreck, boundless and bare,
  The lone and level sands stretch far away."

Just look at the evocative beauty of the phrase "lone and level sands" with its repeated "l" sound (Shelley here employs a type of alliteration known as consonance; the effect is subtle, whilst in the hands of a mediocre poet alliteration is frequently overdone— as Shakespeare parodied in *Love's Labours Lost*). Or take Shelley's decision to employ "Ozymandias", the Hittite name for the Pharaoh Ramses II, as it is so (faintly ridiculously) orotund. Then the way he sets up his hatchet-job, for, as Moses found, in ancient Egypt hot air arose not only from the desert but also from the autocrats. The lines that quote the boast of Ozymandias are so booming and bombastic, punctured then by the devastating simplicity of the phrase "Nothing beside remains."

ii

Readers will be forgiven for skipping the following section, as it contains some strenuous technical stuff—though a quotation from *Hamlet* provides a convenient bridge to the final section of the essay, on the language of prayer.

To demonstrate how the technical analysis of poetry can help us get to the heart of a matter, I begin with an example from Shakespeare's *Macbeth*. The play begins with the three witches chanting "Fair is foul and foul is fair"—"dum-di-dum-di-dum-di-dum" or, more properly speaking, trochaic trimeter with catalexis. A little later we see Macbeth, on his way to his first meeting with the witches. Because the weather is awful, but because a battle has just been won, he says to his friend Banquo: "So fair and foul a day I have not seen." The "di-dum-di-dum-di-dum" (basically iambic) rhythm here is different from that of the witches' chant, much closer to the pattern of everyday speech. But an alert audience will pick up on the words "fair" and "foul" and realise (the alliteration, the repeated "f" sound, helps) that his words are those previously used by the witches. It is very important that the audience gets this, because it is one of the ways Shakespeare tells us that the witches don't *cause* Macbeth to commit terrible crimes; the wickedness is already inside him and (as they are Satanic) the witches draw this out and lead him to turn desire into deed (at one point they cackle gleefully: "By the pricking of my thumbs, something wicked this way comes", since, as servants of Satan, they rejoice in his wickedness).

Shakespeare was extremely astute when it came to the themes of wickedness, guilt, forgiveness. One of the few moments in *Hamlet* when we feel pity for the fratricide Claudius is when he laments: "My words fly up, my thoughts remain below: Words without thoughts never to heaven go" (expressing himself in an iambic couplet, close to the rhythm of everyday speech). This leads to a consideration of the relationship between thoughts, words and prayer, and to the question, which words, what kind of words?

iii

The British government's decision to downgrade the teaching of poetry in schools strongly suggests they have cloth ears. In commenting on the decision, the *Guardian* newspaper noted that "the unresolved, open-minded nature of so much poetry, where meaning has to be extracted from intense engagement with language, is all too appropriate for our present age of uncertainty."

In a time of uncertainty (or, as W.H. Auden put it, an "age of anxiety") prayer is of fundamental importance and, as I shall suggest in the final section of this essay, poetry can provide a perfect vehicle for prayer.

As a latecomer to faith (with Father Ian Corbett as one of my spiritual guides) and as an academic specialising in African literature, including, of course, poetry, I find I am acutely self-conscious when it comes to prayer—in particular, regarding the words I am using. This is in one respect a bad thing—as another spiritual guide, Genevieve Cannan would advise me, involving too much head and too little heart. In another respect, though, I believe that this self-consciousness is salutary, as I shall suggest at the end of this essay. And it suggests a bond between the language of poetry and the language of prayer, for as poets such as T.S. Eliot and W.H. Auden have reminded us, precision is a hallmark of fine poetry. Nowhere more so than in poetry is the search for the right word in the right place so crucial.

For some years, I concluded my devotions by reciting the Lord's Prayer, memorized ever since the confusing experience of school assembly. The words would roll out—by rote—with virtually no attention paid to them by me (I trust that the good Lord was all ears).

I failed to notice the beauty of such lines as "Hallowed be thy name". I also failed to pick up on lines that surely don't work as they should. I have now revised those lines (for I have never been backwards in coming forwards). After "Forgive us our trespasses" I no longer say "As we forgive them that trespass against us", because, sadly, I fail to do so. I am consistently guilty of harbouring grudges (once again, in his *Inner Voice of Love*, Henri Nouwen is wonderful on this topic). So I say, "Guide us into forgiving those who trespass against us."

More crucially—though I may be missing out on a point of theology here—I baulk at the line "Lead us not into temptation." Are we not addressing ourselves to the Lord? And He leads us to salvation, not temptation. So, I say "Let no-one nor any thing lead us into temptation."

Of course, not all prayer employs poetic language. An example is the following, reproduced from Nicky Gumbel's *Why Jesus?* (Alpha International, 1997), which appeals owing to the absolute straightforwardness of its language:

> Lord Jesus Christ, I am sorry for the things I have done wrong in my life (*take a few moments to ask His forgiveness for anything in particular that is on your conscience*). Please forgive me. I now turn from everything that I know is wrong. Thank you that you died on the cross for me so that I could be forgiven and set free.
> Thank you that you offer me forgiveness and the gift of your Spirit. I now receive that gift.
> Please come into my life by your Holy Spirit to be with me forever.
> Thank you, Lord Jesus. Amen.

So simple and so powerful. But to return to my main topic, the language of poetry in relation to the language of prayer: about a year ago another of my spiritual mentors, Ed Evans, with whom I attended the Alpha course, sent me a prayer card, with a Marian prayer that rapidly became my favourite, on account of its meaningfulness, its strength in aiding mindfulness, and—very importantly—the beauty of its language. Here it is:

> Holy Spirit, Lord and giver of life
> who didst overshadow Mary
> that she might become the
> Mother of Jesus our Saviour;
> do thou likewise work silently
> in my heart
> to form within me the fulness of His redeemed
> and redeeming humanity:
> give me a share in his loving heart
> to burn with love for God
> and love for men;
> give me a share in His joy and
> His sorrow,
> His weakness and His strength,
> His labour for the world's salvation.
> And may Mary, blessed among women,
> Mother of our Saviour, pray for me;
> that Christ may be formed in me;
> that I may live in union of heart and will
> with Jesus Christ, her Son,
> our Lord and Saviour. Amen.

I should like to draw readers' attention to some of the most beautiful recognitions, beautifully worded, in that prayer. First there is the startling word-choice— "overshadow"—in the second line. Then the use of parallelism (repetition with variation) in the phrase "His redeemed and / redeeming humanity" and once again (with "loving", "love" and "love") in the three lines that follow. In the first of those lines there is also the arresting, Hopkins-like, use of the verb "burn." Finally, there is the beautiful turn in the last six lines of the prayer, when the addressee becomes not the Holy Spirit, as hitherto, but Mary.

In short, this is a prayer that enables the joy we find through faith, by accessing one of the greatest of our God-given gifts, poetic language. A perfect example of poetry in the service of prayer.

Chapter Postscript: Amy Carmichael and *Rose from Brier*

Shortly after completing this chapter I was discussing my interest in the language of poetry in relation to the language of prayer with Andy Nash, Evangelist at the church I attend, namely, Christchurch Westbourne, Bournemouth. A little later he presented me with a book that had been languishing on the church bookshelves, unborrowed, for years. This turned out to be a tattered old thing but rather sweet (just like me): *Rose from Brier* by Amy Carmichael, which was published in London by the SPCK (Society for the Promotion of Christian Knowledge) in 1957.

Miss Amy Wilson Carmichael was a prominent member of the Dohnavur Fellowship, which, Google informs me, is "a Christian Organization that works towards holistic development, running projects across the area of Child Development." Dohnavur is a village near the tip of South India. At the time of writing *Rose from Brier* Carmichael was an invalid, bed-bound after a serious fall and crippled with arthritis. She had published sixteen previous books.

The publisher's blurb to *Rose from Brier* notes "Miss Carmichael was inspired to write this book by reflecting that most books of comfort for sick people are written by the well, and so miss the mark. Out of long-continued suffering this book has emerged." The book comprises a sequence of letters written for the Dohnavur Foundation's invalids' league, the letters being interspersed with poems / songs. The authorship of the latter isn't stipulated, though some are recognizably by the Psalmist. Others, I guess, are by Carmichael herself. In one letter ("How Songs Came") she talks about the pleasure that songs give her when she happens upon them: "They came not of set purpose, but because I could not help 'taking' them, as the children say; they always think of songs and music too, as something for which we put out our hand, as it were, and 'take.'"

In the letters she quotes poems by Christina Rossetti and Robert Herrick. In the latter instance she says "And He talks with us in many ways, sometimes through the pleasure of rarely quoted old words, like those from Herrick, who, when in 1647 his all was taken from him, wrote:

> God, when he takes my goods and chattels hence,
> Gives me a portion, giving patience:

What is God is God; if so it be
He patience gives, He gives himself to me."

I like that phrase "the pleasure of rarely quoted old words." Herrick's words do give us pleasure, because they are so well chosen and placed; I especially enjoy the boldness of the phrase "What is God is God." The poetry of Herrick gives us pleasure, but the language of poetry here is deployed in the service of faith.

Then there is a passage that suggests Carmichael wrote some (many?) of the songs that are interspersed with the letters. The passage is worth quoting for reasons that lie beyond the realm of literary detective work.

"So the songs came. For by reason of the 'interior sweetness', as Richard Rolle says, 'I was impelled to sing what before I had only said' to Him who hears the least little song of love. Such a song need not look for words, though sometimes the search for the right word can be strangely refreshing. Songs without words are songs to Him."

I want to draw attention to that observation "sometimes the search for the right word can be strangely refreshing." Searching for the right word in writing my chapters in this book was not exactly refreshing, more of a duty. But poetry is different, its language is different; that phrase "the search for the right word" brings us back to T.S. Eliot's comments on the nature of poetic language. And how much more refreshing—water from a sweet well—when poetic language is sourced in the service of prayer, worship, faith.

Now, at the risk of turning this section of this book into a personal diary, I want to draw attention to a prayer from Elizabeth Ruth Obbard's *A Walsingham Prayer Book* (which I received recently as a gift from Ian Corbett). I focus on the lines "Bring home the feet that far from Thee have wandered; / The minds that all but Thee all day have pondered." These lines have become my personal prayer mantra, since: first, they articulate so well my failings (so they act as a *mea culpa*) and, second, I love the poetic audacity of the second line, with the ominous knell of the repeated "all." Whoever wrote these lines, s/he was a distinguished poet.

4

Poems Of Love And Loss

Ian Corbett

These short poems were written upon losing Tashi, as described in the main text. They helped me to grieve, but they also resonate with my thoughts on prayer and are therefore included here. I acknowledge my indebtedness to Schubert's song cycle ' Winterreise' to poems by Wilhelm Muller — which would be a good further exploration for readers of this text.

THE DOOR

You shut the door.
I was left alone – numb, frozen.
'And you held me and there were no words
And there was no time and you held me'.
Time now stretches to infinity but is
Empty, silent, without expectation.
No-one to accompany me, without
weighing thoughts, or
measuring words.
I was too old. You were too young.
And what we had always avoided mentioning

had to come.
The breaking – your breaking out,
my breaking open,
breaking.
You had to go, I knew that, and
I had let you go.
Your future is with another
While I have no future
Because you have gone
And shut the door.

THE HOUSE

I trudge through the darkness of the night,
Face grimly turned to the biting wind,
the clinging rain,
Bound for nowhere, anywhere.
I pass a tiny cottage, its lit, snug interior
visible through unshuttered windows.
I think I see you there, through the driving
rain,
reclining with your customary elegance,
perhaps awaiting supper from your new lover.
I press on. I cannot stop.
No place for me to rest my head
Only the journey.
I can't go on, I must go on.

THE CROWS

Nature falls silent as I tread the rocky
path.
Daffodils and bluebells drop their heads
as I pass.
The birds, songless now, perch aloft,
indifferent to my presence.
Only a lone robin marks my route, until
A screeching of rooks intimidate him,
and
threaten me,
croaking, 'outsider',
'derelict',
'shunned',
Before flying on and leaving me alone,
lonely,
lost.

THE YOUTH

A flaxen-haired youth steps out of the
trees
barefoot, dancing, rejoicing in his
lissom body
and the passing sunlight of a late spring
day.
I sense only the cold of it, and the
endless trail ahead.
'Share my joy', he says,
'I can leap high and touch the clouds.
I can offer you my innocence, and
the warmth of my body'.
But joy is lost to me,
The comforting bed of the lover forever
denied.
I shrug him off, and
Head towards the darkening sky,
the mirage of a future,
the dying world,
Bearing always the aching pain that is all
I have of you.

JOURNEY'S END

I stand alone on the shore
Awed by the immensity of the heaving ocean.
The fat, clouded sun hesitates,
sinks
As a silver sliver of moon arises.
Is this the end?
Do I walk on into the waves
and snuff out life
by becoming one with them,
a Buddhist consummation?
Or do I wait still
for the god to show himself,
the one whose humble, fleeting annunciation
had once inspired but
then deserted me,
the one who habitually hides in darkness,
the one whose presence is felt more in absence,
in intimation,
in suggestion?
Nothing.
Stillness.
Dusk.
I step into the water…
Then…
A whisper of a breeze.
I wait.

Will he come, he who could assuage my hurt?
Perhaps not in the majesty of the setting sun,
Nor in the singing of the sea
But in a quietness deep inside me.
Something draws me back.
I wait again…
Then I turn
To retrace the steps of my suffering,
To return, and
This time to look within rather than without
for a way forward if not for answer
for my restless, wounded soul.
I still wait
But a rumour of angels sustains me.

Ian Corbett and Chris Dunton

5
Was And Is

Reflections on the passing of time, and further reflections on language and on poetic language in the service of faith.

Chris Dunton

i

In H.G. Wells's *The Time Machine* (not just a sci-fi thriller, by the way, but a novel that probes serious questions), when the chief Morlock confronts the time traveller he / it comments: "The problem with you humans is that you cannot come to terms with the difference between was and is."

The way the past impacts on the present—the gulf between the two, or the disruption caused by the one impacting on the other, is of course a central preoccupation of creative writing and perhaps especially of the novel. One only has to think of Dickens or Proust or Faulkner. And it is a major theme of a work by African-American author Brandon Taylor, whose novel *Real Life* was shortlisted for the 2020 Booker Prize. The central character of the novel is a young man who has escaped a wretched childhood in Alabama for a career in science at a northern university. At one point he muses (and *Real Life* is at one level a highly cerebral novel): "when you go to another place you don't have to carry the past with you. You can lay it down . . . There comes a time when you have to stop being who you were, when you have to let the past stay where it is, frozen and impossible. You have to let it go, if you're going to keep moving, if you're going to survive, because the past doesn't need a future. It has no use for what comes next. The past is greedy, always swallowing you up, always taking. If you don't hold it back, if you don't dam it up, it will spread and take and drown."

To return to the quotation with which this chapter began, for the atheistic Wells the gulf between "was" and "is" seemed a critical problem; for the Christian, who believes "In the end is my beginning" it is a problem, but one that can be overcome. In an earlier chapter I cited Henri Nouwen's wonderful book *The Inner Voice of Love*, which guides us not towards trying to discard our past, with all its pain and losses, but towards placing it in perspective through the embrace of redemption. Just now I quoted T.S. Eliot's line "In my end is my beginning"—and Eliot will feature prominently in this chapter—that is to say, everything that leads up to one's end—one's earthly life—is preparation for, and a testing ground for, one's true beginning, unity with one's Maker. Here—and having used the phrase "one's Maker"—I cannot resist inserting an anecdote. When Winston Churchill was on his death-bed—in and out of coma—at a point he came to and said to his wife, Clementine, who was sitting at his bedside: "My dear, I am ready to meet my Maker." Then he added: "It is another matter whether my Maker is ready for the appalling experience of meeting me."

To return to "was" and "is", to the fear of the weight of the past, Christian faith also embraces the weight of the future. I remember taking issue with an obnoxious tour guide in Peru when, in a church in Cuzco, he pointed to paintings made hundreds of years before by converts amongst Quechua (native Americans). One of these paintings was of the nativity and the guide drew our attention to the fact the artist had painted a crucifix hanging from the lintel of the stable and commented that the artist was too ignorant to understand that this was "absurd", that a representation of the death of Christ could not have been present and visible at his birth, thirty-three years before the historical event. I scolded him, referring to the principle of immanence: that the death of Christ is there in his birth, that the one is not fully meaningful without the other. Here, "was" and (in the richest sense) "to be" are indissolubly welded, and "is" can stand for the aspiration to achieve, or the achievement of, faith.

A little above, I noted that our earthly life is but a preparation for and a "testing ground" for our heavenly life. By "testing ground" I was edging towards an extremely complex issue, but one that I believe underlies the whole of this book. That is, the relationship between faith and works. What works for the general good, for the welfare of our fellow beings (not only human) does one perform during the earthly life I have described as a "testing ground" and how do these works relate to the primary duty of faith? This is a difficult issue that I am assured can be addressed in part by immersion in the Epistle of St. James. But it is an issue to be opened up another day, in another book.

ii

In what will, I am afraid, and as our readers will already have gleaned, be an even more than characteristically rambling chapter, I wish to discuss ends and beginnings and to edge towards some further comments on the language of poetry in the service of faith. All of this within a matrix that has to do with the passing of time, something I and my co-author are acutely aware of. For, as Herbert Read put it in his brilliant parody of T.S. Eliot, "as we grow older, we do not get any younger."
Shortly after I completed my earlier chapter in this book, my mother died. She was 102, bedridden, a bag of bones, and had full-blown dementia. When I visited her two days before her death, she was in a dreadful, pitiable state. For all who knew her, the news that the Lord had finally taken her to Him was a source of relief and thankfulness.

Although we never discussed the matter, my

mother evidently had no very strong religious conviction, though whether she would have regarded herself as agnostic or atheist I do not know. Her funeral service was designed as, and programmed as "A celebration of the life of…" One family friend—a devout Christian—who attended the event was distressed that it was "merely secular." My responsibilities were to write and deliver a eulogy and to choose a poem for the celebrant to read out. For reasons having to do with family history, I chose an excerpt from T.S. Eliot's "East Coker", a poem on faith. Some of those attending told me they found the excerpt from Eliot's poem practically impenetrable, but I shall try to open it up a little during the latter part of this chapter.

Some of the afore-mentioned family history now, drawing together the thematic strands of material I am somewhat circuitously heading towards.

When my father was dying, in 1993, I headed home from Lima, Peru, where I was then based and, when he died, at my mother's request sat with her and a local Church of England vicar to plan his funeral service. My mother made a point of requesting we sing a particular hymn, which I shall leave unidentified, so as not to hurt any reader's feelings. She stated this was my father's favourite hymn—as far as I know, a complete fib.

In a strong hymn or spiritual (think of "Amazing Grace" or "God our help in ages past") neither the words nor the music should be facile. The hymn chosen for my father's funeral had always struck me as resembling a tinsel dingle-dangle, its words and its music cheap and tawdry. In a fine work both words and music should arrest the attention, grip the soul; think of the cantatas of J.S. Bach or works by Benjamin Britten such as his Hymn to St. Cecilia, where the marvellous inventiveness and serenity of Britten's music are combined with the words of a great poet, W.H. Auden.

iii

To proceed with matters of faith, words and song, there have been several false starts in my journey towards faith. When I was six or seven years old, my parents suggested I attend Sunday school. This might have been a cunning ruse to get me out of the house on Sunday morning, but I believe it was more a matter of feeling I should be introduced to Christian worship and make up my own mind (or, more properly speaking, heart) about the matter. The woman who conducted the school turned out to be extremely good-natured and expert at communicating with infants; she was also tiny and sported a moustache. At my first session she introduced me to the other kids and asked me if I'd like to sign a song. I guess she had in mind a hymn, but I immediately launched into "Daisy, Daisy, give me your answer do", in what I'm sure was a fair imitation of a Cockney accent. This performance was greeted by the other kids with a combination of frowns and giggles.

It can only get worse. At secondary school, when it came to the haul up to 'O'-levels I registered for an optional subject, Religious Knowledge (in retrospect, I wish I'd gone for another option, ancient Greek). My motive for doing so had nothing, I'm ashamed to say, with some germinal inclination towards faith, but because I thought it would be neat to bag ten 'O'-levels rather than the statutory nine. The teacher for the subject was an amiable old man who rejoiced in the nickname Amos. I'm sure he did a good job, but my 'O'-levels results slip shows that for Religious Knowledge I came in with an 'H' grade, the most dismal level of fail achievable. Oh vanity, all is vanity. I've described elsewhere in this book how, when I relocated to the UK in 2016, I eventually came to faith. Since writing my earlier chapters I have changed accommodation and, hence, churches. In my previous church I would gaze lovingly at a stained-glass window depicting the return of the prodigal son (a beautifully executed, tender work of art, apart from the standard Disneyland castle in its background). In my new church I gaze at a tapestry triptych, the panels of which read "Christ died. Christ has risen. Christ will come again." Familiar words, of course, voicing a central concept, but I have never before been so struck by the radical simplicity of the language, by the effect of the move from a past tense verb to present perfect to future (died—has risen—will come), and by how powerful this is. Which brings us neatly back to ideas of the passing of time (so central to this chapter) and of the essence of poetic language, and to the use of poetic language in the service of faith.

iv

Why did I choose an excerpt from T.S. Eliot's "East Coker" to be read at my mother's service? I knew full well how difficult some of those attending would find it. My reason was in recall of an especially fine day out with my mother when, years before, her favourite nephew had driven down from his home in Bearsden, near Glasgow, to spend a few days visiting relatives in Poole and Bournemouth, and took me and my mother and father out for a day trip in his car. I requested that, inter alia, we visit the village of East Coker, not too far away from home, in south Somerset. I told my parents and cousin that this is where T.S. Eliot's ancestors came from and that one of his major poems was named after the village, a revelation that was not greeted with wild enthusiasm. I had scribbled out the relevant part of the poem "East Coker" to recite as we reached the steep, narrow road that leads down to the village. Popular acclaim still proved elusive. In the village church the mood improved, as I located an oval plaque commemorating Eliot, a beautiful work depicting a dove and lines from "Little Gidding", another of the *Four Quartets* of which "East Coker" forms a part. I can't remember if the plaque quotes the whole quatrain (four-line stanza), or only its first line, in which case (always happy to show off) I would have recited the rest from memory. Here it is:

> The dove descending breaks the air
> With flame of incandescent terror
> Of which the tongues declare
> The one discharge from sin and error.

My cousin, wide-eyed, exclaimed "fearsome words", to which I responded "or one could say, awe-inspiring." At which point we headed off for lunch.

This brings me back to the subject of the language of poetry and the role of poetry in the service of faith. Eliot's early poetry was written during, and indeed played a pivotal role in, the growth of the modernist period. The nature of much of it is perhaps best exemplified by lines from "The Love Song of J. Alfred Prufrock": "The evening is laid out against the sky / Like a patient etherized upon a table." The first of these lines leads one to expect the completion of a conventional romantic lyric, an expectation that is blown apart by the following line. I remember organizing a poetry workshop at the National University of Lesotho, at which the guest speaker was an American professor of poetry of a highly conservative disposition when it came to the nature of poetic language. One of the students recited a short piece by the American modernist e.e.cummings [sic], who was more-or-less contemporary with Eliot, at the end of which the Professor declared "That's fun. But it's not a poem." He then went on to critique the modernist movement, for which he appeared to hold Eliot culpable.

In the professor's view a poem must be set out in stanzas, it should have a regular rhythm (a metrical pattern) and rhyme and other traditional devices.

The fourth section of "East Coker" is a short piece divided into five quintets or five-line stanzas. The first of these reads as follows:

> The wounded surgeon plies the steel
> That questions the distempered part;
> Beneath the bleeding hands we feel
> The sharp compassion of the healer's art
> Reading the enigma of the fever chart."

Not exactly an easy ride, those lines, with their challenging word-choice and their vision of the surgeon as a Christ-like figure. But in other ways they are poetically highly traditional, even down to the use of an ABABB rhyme scheme ("steel" and "feel" as A).

v

Before I round off by returning to "East Coker" I want to make use of a line from a poem by George Herbert. A note on that poet first. Herbert (1563-1633) was Welsh-born and a clergyman in the Church of England. His small but wonderful poetic output nearly all comprised work exploring and expressing Christian faith. He differs in this respect from his better-known near-contemporary John

Donne (1572-1631). Donne was also a clergyman (Dean of St. Paul's) but wrote both poetry on faith (the famous Holy Sonnets, some of which were set to superb music by Benjamin Britten) and also poetry on other topics, including secular love poems.

The line of Herbert I am focussing on reads "Is all beauty in a winding stair?" This refers to Herbert's conviction that plain speaking may be as much a hallmark of fine poetry as devices such as rhyme, alliteration and ornamental language. And that brings us back to Eliot's observation, quoted in an earlier chapter, that what makes a poem a poem is the very intimate (and yet often complex, challenging) way the words of the poem interrelate, lean upon each other, depend upon each other. Devices such as rhyme and alliteration are there for a poet to make use of, or choose not to.

When asked to select a poem for the celebrant to read at my mother's life celebration, I opted for the final twenty lines of Eliot's "East Coker." These read as follows:

> Home is where one starts from. As we grow older
>   The world becomes stranger, the pattern more complicated
> Of dead and living. Not the intense moment
> Isolated, with no before and after,
> But a lifetime burning in every moment
> And not the lifetime of one man only
> But of old stones that cannot be deciphered.

There is a time for the evening under starlight,
A time for the evening under lamplight
(The evening with the photograph album).
Love is most nearly itself
When here and now cease to matter.
Old men ought to be explorers
Here or there does not matter
We must be still and still moving
Into another intensity
For a further union, a deeper communion
Through the dark cold and the empty
desolation,

The wave cry, the wind cry, the vast waters
Of the petrel and the porpoise. In the end is
my beginning.

These lines tease out an argument that leads to the closing statement "In my end is my beginning", a line that echoes earlier phrases in what is a long (211-line) and highly demanding poem. In the lines I have quoted Eliot uses virtually no traditional devices of the kind I have cited above. Until one gets to the last few lines, that is, when in an unforgettable image of desolation, he employs alliteration (the "w" of "wave", "wind" and "waters", the "p" of "petrel" and "porpoise" and the sequence of "s" sounds). The alliterative words are bound together by the approximate rhyme of "waters" and "porpoise". Some readers might remark "but I didn't notice any of that happening." Precisely. In Eliot's hands poetic technique does not draw attention to itself.

In this chapter, I have expanded upon my earlier chapter in the light of my mother's death and her life celebration, which occurred after that chapter was written. I have spent time discussing the technicalities of poetry, because that is part of my professional training and responsibility, part of what I *do*. I have written about poetry in the service of faith, because living in and from faith is where I now trust I *am*.

Ian Corbett and Chris Dunton

6

Love At The Centre Of Abandonment

Ian Corbett

i

A REPLY TO MYSELF

This book was begun at the start of the Covid-19 pandemic in 2020 and has suffered an interrupted history. It is now 2022 and the end of the pandemic is in sight, or at least the stage where we can learn to live with it. I find my perceptions and understanding have evolved in that time. I started to write in the immediate aftermath of Tashi and I deciding our ways must diverge, and it was still a very raw experience. When I read that record now, my reactions seem rather bleak and severe. I don't retract any of those reactions but I now see them in a larger prospective. I hope that, in responding to my earlier self, my observations will help those who have trodden a similar path and may now be re-assessing their attitudes.

It has taken me all of these two years to fully come to terms with my new relationship with Tashi. The utter grief and desolation lasted much longer than I had anticipated, and I was daily in tears, feeling utterly lost. Not least owing to his constant kindness and understanding, I am now at a stage when I can be in his presence, with Patrick, without feeling my aloneness so acutely, and I have learned gradually to let him go, little by little, until we have settled into the sort of sustained, passionate friendship that is also acceptable to Patrick. Tashi can remain a great strength to me, and I can also appreciate with greater equanimity all the love he gave me, and which he still gives me but in a different way. I have learned it is possible to adjust! I sometimes even think, shall I meet someone else, even though Tashi is irreplaceable? Probably not in my eightieth year! But life is more balanced and bearable. I now realise that, in writing as I did earlier, I gave the impression that relationships are innately hostile to spiritual growth, a barrier to giving self away in a higher vocation. I think for some people this is true, but for most of us relationships are a venue for discovering God, who, as we have said, is love. Many marital relationships grow in holiness the one with the other. But there is a sense in which ultimately we are all alone: we never know each other completely, and we all meet death alone. I wanted to stress this stark aspect of our growth towards God towards the end. But, of course, it is not the whole story.

Nor is my earlier assertion that we have to be stripped down for spiritual growth because the question follows, stripped down for what? To enter the dazzling darkness of Godself certainly, but we may then be guided or driven to expand ourselves in some sort of service in hitherto unexpected ways: our spiritual nakedness is not an end in itself. By being a little kinder to myself than I possibly was earlier, I can recognise that my spiritual prescription still leaves me with a deep sadness, bordering on depression, and an inner restlessness that I have not accounted for. It is partly the lack of the lover, also a deeper identification with the terrible needs of our world in its present dangerous, if not terminal, condition – climate change, the extinction of species, pollution, increasing warfare, ethnic cleansing, human slavery – but also an unfulfilled search for myself, who I am, that is more urgent now for, as a retired person, I can no longer define myself in terms of my work. I yearn for the stillness that such a quest might yield.

This is an elusive occupation because, as already explored, the God in whom I may find fulfilment often seems absent, and there is perhaps a dialectical process to be followed in that finding God, on the one hand, and self on the other, can only proceed in tandem. And there is a harshness in this, because if God has to a degree withdrawn from this world he cannot be experienced as an agent in it. Rowan Williams has argued that 'For the Word to become flesh is for the Word to live in the centre of divine absence – ultimately in death and abandonment. Faith is seeing/sensing the Word as an absolute imperative of love in the hidden centre of the abandoned world'. He goes on to say that the opposite of this demanding faith is not doubt but the illusion that we can play God by finding final solutions that are actually always destructive of humanity. The terrible truth is that God in Christ has offered us a freedom that we cannot cope with. We want answers to the great ambiguities of life but have to realise we can only work towards them by witnessing and living as those who believe in the mystery of God in Christ. We shall never arrive, but the exploration is what life is really about. In confronting it, I do feel the need for greater silence and aloneness, while not being lonely and continuing to value the great gift and comfort of human love and care.

As I reconsider my position, the great conviction that has powered all my ministry reasserts itself alongside my need for greater quiet in my monastic cell – Jesus' call, which was the leitmotiv of his own ministry, to bring 'good news to the poor'. The sermons of Oscar Romero, the martyred Archbishop of El Salvador, originally awakened me to this imperative:-

> 'The guarantee of one's prayer is not in saying a lot of words,
> The guarantee of one's petition is very easy to know:
> How do I treat the poor?
> Because that is where God is.
> The degree to which you approach them
> or the scorn with which you approach them -

that is how you approach God.
What you do to them you do to God.
The way you look at them is the way you look
at God.'

'A religion of Sunday mass but of unjust weeks
does not please the Lord.
A religion of much praying but with hypocrisy
in the heart is not Christian.

A Church that sets itself up only to be
respected,
to have popularity and comfort,
but that forgets to protest against injustice
is not the true Church of our Divine
Redeemer'.

This is because 'human beings are also divine beings'.
The essential connection between believing the faith
(the way of withdrawal and contemplation) and living
the faith (the way of selfless service) he expresses
thus:-

'To each of us Christ is saying:
If you want your life and mission to be fruitful
like mine, do like me.
Be converted into a seed that lets itself be
buried.

Let yourself die. Do not be afraid.
those who shun suffering will remain alone,

No one is more alone than the selfish.
But if you give your life out of love for others,
as I give mine for all, you will reap a great
harvest.'

'We must learn this invitation of Christ:
Those who wish to come after me must
renounce themselves.
Let them renounce themselves,
renounce their comforts,
renounce their prejudices,
and follow only the mind of Christ,
which can lead us to death
but will surely also lead to resurrection'.

'The violence we preach is not the violence of
the sword, the violence of hatred.
It is the violence of love, of brotherhood,
the violence that wills to beat weapons
into sickles for work'.

Pope Francis sums up the conviction that Christ must
be lived as well as known, that the imperative of love
is at the centre, that 'ultimate reality is gracious'
(Paul Tillich) by saying 'The Church should be a body
with the poor at its heart, not just an organisation
with a heart for the poor'. So our private
contemplation of the crucified Jesus should arouse in
us the realisation that we are to be spared nothing. It
is the dilemma of serving the impossible love and
freedom that is offered us: Herbert McCabe

observed that 'if you don't love you'll die, and if you do love they'll kill you'. A retreat into meditation drives me out again into the world. George Appleton, once Bishop of Jerusalem, preached many years ago:

> 'Jesus taught forgiveness. On the cross he lived it… Jesus was never more like God than on the Cross. It has been said that there was a cross in the heart of God before ever there was one or Calvary. It might be added that there will continue to be a cross in the heart of God until the last, lost child comes home to the Father'.

Perhaps loving Tashi, and being loved by him, and the ensuing introspection it has provoked, has taught me how to love more widely again. But I need to recall and act upon the stern advice I gave myself earlier, to nurture the interior life so as to be able to support paying the cost of discipleship in the world.

So I am discovering again that true spirituality is not only about detachment but about engagement, about reconciliation (both within and between ourselves) not division, and about not so much as our finding God but our patiently allowing God to find us. Perhaps Tashi's love has enabled me to be more open, compassionate and expectant. I can live with uncertainty but not without love, in all its many incarnations. I can let go, caring not for my own safety even though negotiating life may be like being lost in a maze. I realise I depend on a fulness as yet unseen, that I cannot fully understand and must wait and trust, believing more will be revealed: it was Job's humility and patience that led him to a deeper understanding *in the end*, having refused to accept easy answers and comfort. And Jacob wrestled with God to arrive at a greater depth of understanding. We can wait for illumination with confidence because on the Cross we can see God's desire to understand us, and in his wounds, we can see the extent of his striving. On all my journeying I now expect to find hedges of thorns but I now also listen for the presence that will show me a path I have never taken, to a door I have never opened – into a rose garden of a new level of awareness.

ii

WHERE AM I NOW?

I started this book with a desire to share my exploration into the meaning of life in a manner that would speak to a wider audience than that of only the Christian or the theist. As I reflect further, and with the passage of time, I find that I am returning slowly to a more precisely Christian prospective, though one renewed and enhanced by my wanderings. I am still constantly excited by discovering the divine in new experiences, whether African or Native American, Himalayan Buddhist or the scientific observations of Einstein. But I realise more and more that I am drawn to express my searching for truth in models based on a Presence from beyond that incarnates itself, breaks into our human life. I hope I will not be drawing too far away from those who feel they must be less closely associated with this model or labelling, and that they will continue to be able to accompany me. All seekers profit from mutual support and creative sharing.

So, as I approach my eightieth birthday, where do I find myself in my 'Vision Quest'? God is certainly more elusive. I like R.S.Thomas' poem about seeking God being like knocking on the door of an old house, receiving no reply, moving away but then looking back and seeing the twitch of a curtain – someone is there. Or his image of our arriving to find God has already departed. So my conviction of divine existence is certainly based more on a sense of absence rather than presence, but that conviction is stronger than ever, owing to 'evidences' gleamed over the years, in music, literature, nature, relationship and vocation. So I am a little more settled, accepting – and expectant. I realise I shall be more alone, and will continue to share in the suffering of Godself, but I am more than ever convinced that that self is love itself, love at the centre of the universe, always trying to find its way in. This assertion is possible, or course, because of the love I have received – from the Presence itself on occasion and from the experience of human ecstasy, not least in my relationship with Tashi. Furthermore, the understanding that this love in its essence is quite beyond our knowing, enables me to face the darkness of the world and my own life with equanimity and a sort of stoic confidence. All WILL be well – in the end (those words again).

So what do I now discern about this love? God's loving us, and enabling us to go on in this challenging and frightening world, is the meaning of our existence. Reality lies in relationships, which are the heart of faith. The African concept of 'ubuntu', togetherness, says 'a person is a person through other persons': we find our fulfilment in God and one another. I believe that God is present, whether detected or not, wherever I have an obligation, where I am committed unconditionally. The opposite of the true religious experience is therefore neglect: ignoring the needs of the other is certainly to move away from God. The two great realities in life are loving and dying, and we must embrace both. We can dare to do so because the Lord of life seeks fellowship with us: incarnate in our lives is the aim of our adoration. One of the Greek words for love is 'eros', the opposite of 'thanatos' (death). It requires effort and struggle. Descartes might have said not 'I think therefore I am' but 'I love therefore I am'. 'God' is the actual symbol of love, life, eternity. Our lostness is usually occasioned by our loving 'disastrously little': we must be hungry for it, as often as in its sexual expression, and we must always be ready to start again. Because this love in its essence is costly. Jesus said, 'Love one another: as I have loved you so are you to love one another'. This love faces even crucifixion. That is why Lear can say 'I have taken too little care of it', and Othello, 'when I love thee not, chaos has come again'. It is the love of which Cleopatra speaks to Anthony when she confesses 'eternity was on our lips'.

I don't believe love comes in graded forms, as described in C.S.Lewis' 'The Four Loves' – love of things, animals, people, God. These various aspects flow into one another. God loves us passionately, in both senses of the word, fervently and sufferingly, and He calls forth nothing less in us. God is love: 'by this (loving) shall all men know you are my disciples'. This, of course, for Christians is the test of church life. It fails it miserably: I remember walking the ramparts of Auckland Castle, then the home of Bishops of Durham, with David Jenkins and his being in tears lamenting that the Church has never learned the meaning of love. In the Church of England, we cannot make up our minds whether sexual minorities are fully human, we are silent in the face of a growing worldwide persecution of Christians, and we spend more and more money on centralisation and bureaucracy – including bishops – so starving parish life where the church should be 'happening'. That is sadly why as I feel my spirituality deepening, I find, outside the sacraments, participation in church life becomes less and less frequent. At best the Church has 'loved wholeheartedly but with too ordinary a heart'. It is certainly an intimidating quality of love that loving but lukewarmly can reveal what is worst in us, our biases against giving and sharing. The greatest aspect of this gift is that it enables us to love people as they are, and not as we would wish them to be. God is constantly trying to stretch our hearts a little wider so we may admit yet others into our lives. I am reminded of the prayer of Michel Quoist, of the 'priest on a Sunday night'. Exhausted after a long and demanding day, the priest complains to God that too many people are invading his life and taking it over. God replies, had not the priest noticed that Jesus himself had slipped in among them? We shall certainly sometimes feel overwhelmed if we open our hearts but love is like a dynamo: the more you expend it the more it seems able to give. An Irish friend of mine once wrote when I was feeling low, 'give what you lack', meaning, I think, keep on trying to love, and love will come. Unremitting love is unconquerable.

In the Gospels, love is presented as a responsibility we must shoulder: its test is our readiness to take sides, as in care of the wounded, hopeless and marginalised. Luke reveals it as a readiness to heal and, in Jesus' washing of the disciples' feet, to forgive – the prerequisite of all reconciliation. But in the Farewell Discourses of St. John's Gospel, we encounter an existential crisis: the love described and offered is almost so beyond our capacity to understand that we constantly fail in living it. This can explain the slow progress and endless struggles of the Early Church, the catastrophes of the Middle Ages (the Inquisition, the Crusades) and the failures of the Church today, alluded to above. It is as though God in Christ has offered us a love and freedom which we cannot handle. It seems clear from the world today that our intellectual capacity has grown far faster than our moral and religious capacities, hence the great dangers we are in. If 'before every human being there walks an angel proclaiming: make way, make way for the image of God', then it seems we have been given a vocation too heavy for us to bear. Yet, according to the author of *The Cloud of Unknowing*, 'unless love passes into acts... it is hypocritical'. The hope must lie in the very persistence of that love at the centre, 'the voice under all silences, the hope which has no opposite in fear'.

One aspect of our difficulty could be that Christians have tended to eschew 'eros' for 'agapé', that is the Greek word usually meaning passionate, human loving over against the rarer word implying disinterested, possibly divine, loving – unattached. My great mentor in times past, Alan Ecclestone, much lauded liberal Christian author, was always keen to point out that agapé needs eros to give it drive and energy, and he used to enjoy telling a version of the life of St. Elizabeth, the patron saint of Hungary, to illustrate this. She lived a princess in twelfth century Budapest, and fell madly in love with Prince Ludwig of Thuringia. He went off on the fifth Crusade, and, as he travelled through Italy, they exchanged the most passionate love letters. He was poisoned while awaiting embarkation at Brindisi, and died. Elizabeth was inconsolable in a frenzy of loss.

Eventually, she became a Franciscan tertiary and devoted herself to the care of the poor of the city. Poverty became the repository of her oceanic love; she even lived in poverty herself. She died within three years, exhausted by her efforts. She was canonised only a few years later, such had been the example of her life. She has revealed the fullness of the love of God. But the significant point is that she was able to offer her life so sacrificially because she had lived so passionately. Eros was the motor of her agape: it was because she had known the passion of human love that she was energised to enlarge this to a wider level. The essence of her humanity was that she was a great lover with a great capacity for self-giving from a generous heart. This is what makes a saint. It is because the Church has divorced eros from agape that it has been such a failure of love. But that is only part of its lack of discernment: its patriarchal structures, centuries of the subjugation of women, institutional racism and persecutions of sexual minorities are other aspects. All these imbalances in love together can even effect social and even international relationships – because, as human beings made in the divine image, our core identity is to love: it is our essence, and the right of everyone to be venerated at least once in a lifetime. Loving is a case of 'carrying on carrying on', for that is our nature and our only response to what would overcome us. It is clear, however, that Christianity has failed to enable love to be our guide, failed to enable eros-agape to energise and transform life.

This is why discussion of the matters of love is plagued with fear and depressed in practice. Reforming church structures is a trivial matter compared to the need to address this. For anger and hatred too often overcome love and creativity.

I mention all these negative aspects of church life because they threaten and undermine all I hold essential to the core of our humanity and to my quest for discovering the grounding of this to be in the Divine Presence that indwells our universe. The love of God and of humans is indivisible: 'eternity is in love with the production of time' (Blake). We can never love too much. Yet the Church has turned positive love into renunciation, accepting uncritically conditions of the time (as with slavery), has mistreated eros, women and the environment, and has undervalued the ancient Christian tradition of friendship. We have to work at ways that enable love to grow. Love means treating all others as equals, affirming them in their own being. Because of our failures in love there is a crisis of belief today – not in faith or doctrine, but in life itself: there is a widespread pessimism and a feeling of impotence. The will to live can fade under sufficient pressure. Love declares that the will to live can be maintained, that there is meaning in life even in the face of death. In a loveless society life is robbed of meaning. But love asserts that God places an infinite value on each and every creature and we must be compassionate trustees of that. Love respects the autonomy of all persons, even the lowliest, and this must never be overridden, even in the pursuit of good. This is the message of the Cross of Jesus, where we see God giving Godself in an undefeated love for us and of Creation.

Such is my attempt to outline the personal Credo at which I have now arrived. In that sense, it is less universal in appeal than my beginning. But I hope the progress of the journey in itself will resonate with and be helpful to some. And, of course, the journey will continue. But I may become too ancient to have the energy to share it with you any further. I can best sum up my deepest, innermost conviction by quoting my hero in the faith, the French priest and palaeontologist, Pierre Teilhard de Chardin:-

'Love is the free and imaginative overflowing
of the Spirit over all unexplored paths.
It links those who live in bonds that unite
but do not destroy,

Causing them to discover in their mutual contact, an exaltation capable of stirring to the very core, of their being all that they possess of uniqueness and creative power.

Love alone can unite living beings
so as to complete and fulfil them,
for it alone joins them by what is deepest in themselves.

All we need is to imagine our ability to love
developing until it embraces the totality
of the people of the Earth'.

He adds:-

'Love is the most powerful
and still the most unknown
energy in the world'…

List of References

P. xix Quotation from *The Shattering of Loneliness*:
Erik Varden

P. xix Text from the *Resurrection Symphony* – Gustav
Mahler

P. xxi St. John Chrysostom – Preface

P. 7 Poem by Madeleine Owen-Williams, 1983,
taken from a cutting from the Church Times, date
unknown

P. 8 *There is Only One Road*: Teilhard de Chardin:

p. 33 *Disturb us, Lord*: Attributed to Sir Francis Drake

p. 35 *Prayer*: George Appleton, taken from a cutting
in *The Daily Telegraph*, date unknown.

P. 36 *Prayer*: George Herbert

p. 42 *Ozymandias*: Shelley

p. 46 *Why Jesus?* Nicky Gumbel's (Alpha
International, 1997)

p. 69-70 *East Coker*: T.S. Eliot:

p. 76 Sermon Extract: Oscar Romero

p. 88 *Love*: Teilhard de Chardin, from *Building the
Earth*

Also by Ian Corbett:- '*A Disreputable Priest*'
Gilead Books Publishing

'You are a disreputable priest; but only a disreputable priest can help me.'

These words spoken to Ian Corbett early in his ministry by a university student were to echo through the years that followed: years that took him into pioneering missionary ministry with people on the edges of their societies in the UK, Africa, Ireland, Canada and the USA. As a gay Anglican priest struggling with 'coming out', Ian has been well placed to support people who are different – whether in sexuality or ethnicity – from the prevailing culture around them.

For over 3 decades I have watched from afar with admiration Ian's pastoral work and deep commitment to marginalised people. This memoir should make an absorbing and enriching read.

> *Revd Professor Michael H. Taylor OBE, Emeritus Professor of Social Theology, University of Birmingham and former Director of Christian Aid*

Ian's lifetime of work in some of the most marginalised, misunderstood and endangered communities marks him out as a Christian priest who has taken his vocation to the limits of geographical and cultural difference. Not for him the comforts of the home counties, rather the rarer and prized satisfaction of insecurity, unpredictability and the unknown in remote, materially poor but spirit-filled communities where opportunities for compassion and empowerment abounded. In both of these he proved generous and gifted to an extraordinary degree.

Revd Richard Kirker, Founder and former CEO, Lesbian and Gay Christian Movement

Other Works by Chris Dunton

Chris Dunton's first three books were all academic texts—one small, two much bigger—on Nigerian drama and theatre, which is one of his major research interests. That is probably all you need to know about that.

Dunton has always been a human rights activist, being, for example, a leading member of Matrix, a group that contests homophobia in Lesotho, and his next book, co-authored with the Finnish scholar Mai Palmberg, was *Human Rights and Homosexualities in Southern Africa*. This was published by the University of Uppsala, Sweden, as one in a series of monographs. The second edition carried words of praise from Peter Nobel, grandson of Alfred. Unaccountably, this did not lead to Dunton and Palmberg being awarded a Prize.

Dunton also writes short stories and a collection of these, set in West Africa and titled *Boxing*, is available from the African Books Collective, Oxford. All readers of the present book are warmly encouraged to purchase a copy, in order to boost Dunton's royalties.

He has three book projects on the boil or being actively considered. One of these will be on faith, the churches and LGBTQ+ identity in Africa (though he doesn't know it yet, maybe Ian Corbett will co-author this). Another is a further collection of short stories, plus travel sketches, drawn from a weekly column Dunton produces for a Lesotho newspaper. The third will be on his current major research interest, Rhetoric Studies applied to African texts. This will be a set of essays, some new, some reprinted, and some co-authored with scholars from Lesotho, Kenya and the UK, that critically examine African examples of rhetoric—in other words texts that employ the language of persuasion: political speeches and election rally songs, contributions to parliamentary debates, newspaper editorials and opinion pieces, advertisements, sermons, public health campaign announcements, and so on.

Other Titles from Pendlebury Press

Christianity and Social Order: William Temple.

This brilliant seminal work, first published in 1942, explores the extent to which the Church and Christians in general have a right to interfere in matters of Society and State. While it counsels against the Church dabbling in party politics, it lays down principles upon which social policies should be founded.

Dare to Break Bread: Geoffrey Howard

"It is a small miracle (but truly a miracle) to read this book" – Trevor Huddleston. The author leaves his inner-city parish to contemplate on the Eucharist at a hermitage in the Sahara Desert. This book presents a challenge to all who break bread in our Lord's name.

Fire in Coventry: Stephen Verney.

Renewal won't happen where you are? You will never see growth? Think again. When one person is open to the Holy Spirit. Wham!

From Death into Life: William Haslam

Converted by his own sermon? And revival spreads

like a bush fire! Reading is believing.

Grace and Mortgage: Peter Selby

Powerful and insightful. A must for all who know something is wrong with our credit-based economy but want to understand what it is and how to change it.

Kidnapped (annotated): 2019 Edition: Robert Louis Stephenson

Kidnapped was rated number 24 in the 100 best novels of all time by the UK's *Guardian* Newspaper, which declared it to be a masterpiece, a thrilling adventure story and gripping history, and carries a message for the 21st century. This edition is annotated with explanation of over a hundred Scottish expressions that have disappeared from common use.

Look for the Living: Peter Selby

Within years of the life of Jesus, his resurrection was believed by those who had never seen him. How? A fascinating, in-depth, scholarly analysis.

New Springtime – New Life for the Anglican-Catholic

Movement: Geoffrey Squire

In recent years, the Anglo-Catholic movement has taken a bruising. In this book, Geoffrey Squire SSC gives new hope to those who subscribe to that churchmanship.

Outrageous Grace: Ron Wood

"This is the story of the Secret Gospel - the Good News that is so outrageous the church doesn't want you to hear it. It is the gospel that Jesus preached."

Readings in St. John's Gospel: William Temple

A masterpiece. A devotional and scholarly classic. Currently, we can only offer this for Kindle, in UK, but are negotiating paperback rights. You should be able to order it from Amazon.com in the USA.

Stretcher Bearer – A Worcestershire Regiment Soldier's WW1 Notebook: George Howard

This is a transcript of George A Howard's WW1 notebook, which was found by his grandson in 2013. This is no grand work of literature, nor does it cover more than 15 months of the war. The many rough edges and omissions have not been edited out, but it shows details of a soldier's life that is rarely seen.

Tantalisingly, the notebook shows signs of previous ownership by a German soldier. Who was he?

The Bible As Comedy: Albert Radcliffe

Invaluable for preachers and those wanting to see the Bible afresh. Though this book will make you smile, it is 350 pages of serious exegesis. It is not a joke book. The author borrows the Greek meaning of comedy as being the opposite of tragedy. The book is well structured and can be used as a work of reference as well as being a fascinating page turner.

Through Lent With Loyola: Donald Nicholson

This daily devotional guide through Lent, Holy Week and Easter Week, is a "Distillation of The Spiritual Exercises of Ignatius Loyola."

The Unutterable Beauty: G.A Studdert Kennedy

These poems are largely from the First World War. In their simplicity, they touch the hearts of all who read them. Their vivid portrayal of the futility of war and of the humanity of those engaged in it makes them rank among the poems of Rupert Brooke, Wilfrid Owen and Siegfried Sassoon.

Weep Not For Me: Geoffrey Howard

These Stations of the Cross are illustrated by events

in Jerusalem and the author's city of Salford.

Wheelbarrow Across The Sahara: Geoffrey Howard (100% of our profit and of the author's royalty goes to) the Water For Kids charity

This is the Reverend Geoffrey Howard's gripping account of pushing a Chinese wheel-barrow, a gruelling 2000 miles from Beni Abbes in Algeria, to Kano in Nigeria. Chris Bonington wrote that it is compulsive reading. Humphrey Carpenter said that it is the most extraordinary contemporary travel book he had ever read.

Who Moved The Stone: Frank Morison

Even though this is otherwise out-of-print in UK, we can publish this only in USA because of rights issues. However, you should be able to order it from Amazon.com

.

Printed in Great Britain
by Amazon